W9-DDG-068

Weather on the Move

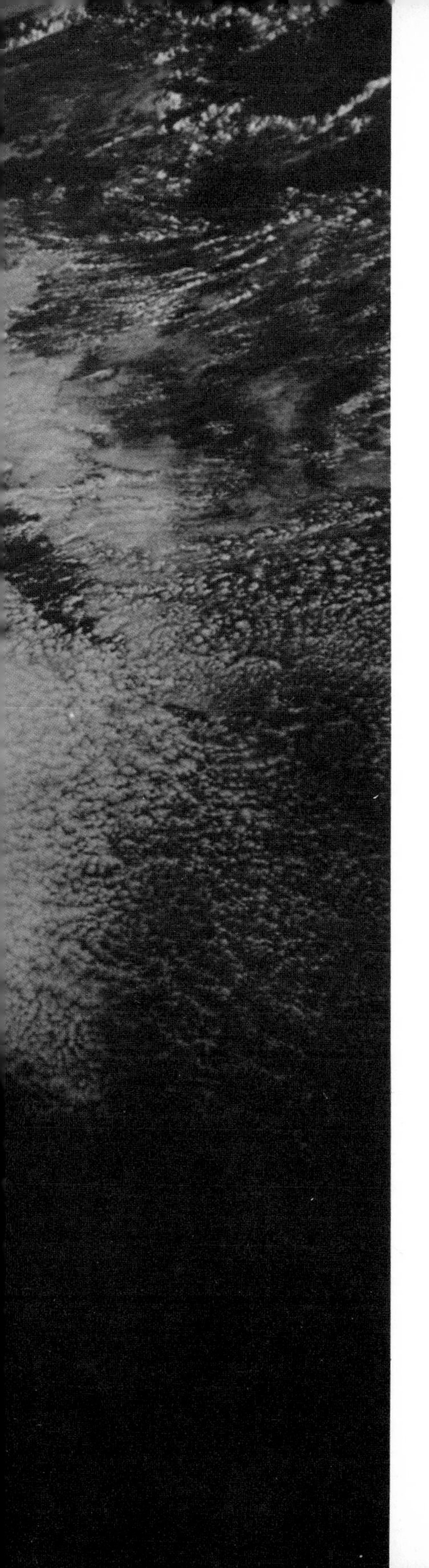

Weather on the Move

BY

Eve Marie Iger

ILLUSTRATED WITH

Photographs & Drawings

NEW YORK

Young Scott Books

To my father,
Ing. Joseph Sperling
of Mexico City,
who made me aware of the chemistry of the air.

★

ACKNOWLEDGMENTS

Sincere thanks to Professor James E. Miller, Chairman of the Department of Meteorology, New York University, who guided the direction of this book; and to the Environmental Science Services Administration, Department of Commerce, parent organization of the United States Weather Bureau, whose National Meteorological Center at Suitland, Maryland, provided much of the information for this book.

Library of Congress Catalog Card No. 78-120945
Printed in U.S.A.

TABLE OF CONTENTS

1. Air on the Go 7

Weather Moves

2. Forces Aloft 18

Temperature

Humidity

Pressure

3. Patterns of Weather 32

Winds

Air Masses

Clouds

Thunderstorm Brewing

Hurricane Country

4. Man's Control of Weather 53

Rain, Rain Go Away

World Weather Watch

Follow the Weather

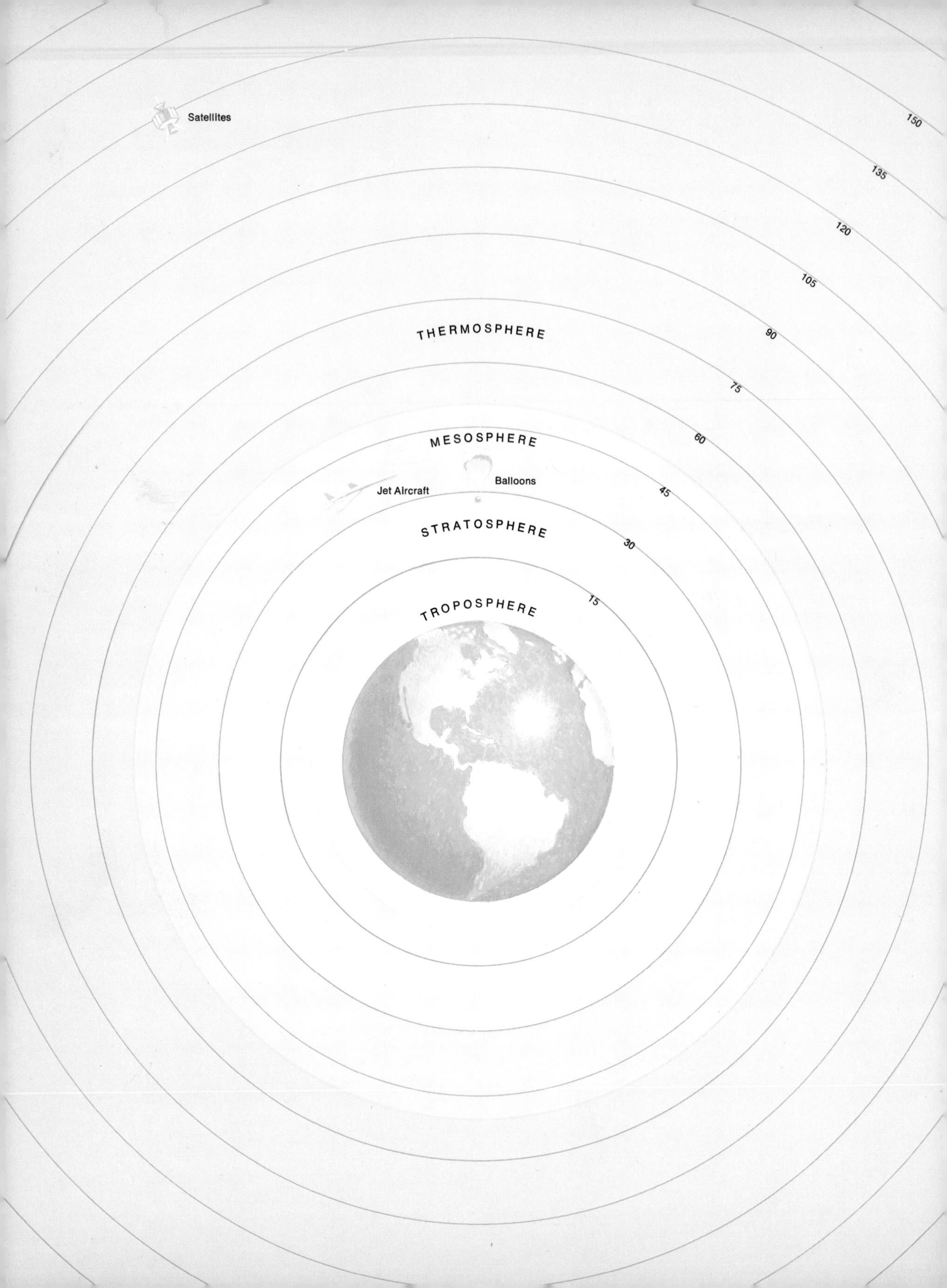
Satellites
150
135
120
105
THERMOSPHERE
90
75
MESOSPHERE
60
Balloons
Jet Aircraft
45
STRATOSPHERE
30
TROPOSPHERE
15

1. Air on the Go

Weather Moves

Our good earth with its cloud cover is like a bright marble in space. That is what a moonbound earthling said as he traveled hundreds of thousands of miles in space. There is no weather where astronauts go. But weather is very important in the planning of moon shot launchings and splashdowns. In fact, weather affects most things men do.

The earth is wrapped in a thin, invisible veil of air. All the air around the earth is called the ATMOSPHERE—"sphere of breath," in Greek. Scientists do not agree how far this veil of air extends. But the first five-to-ten mile layer of the vast atmosphere is where the weather action is.

TROPOSPHERE is the name of this narrow region of weather action. *Tropos* is Greek for "turning." This, then, is the turning-sphere of air. Keep that in mind. It will help you understand the changes overhead.

Gravity, the earth's pulling power, traps about 85% of all air and almost all water-in-air into the troposphere, the sphere of constantly turning, mixing, swirling movement. It is this restlessness of air that is weather change.

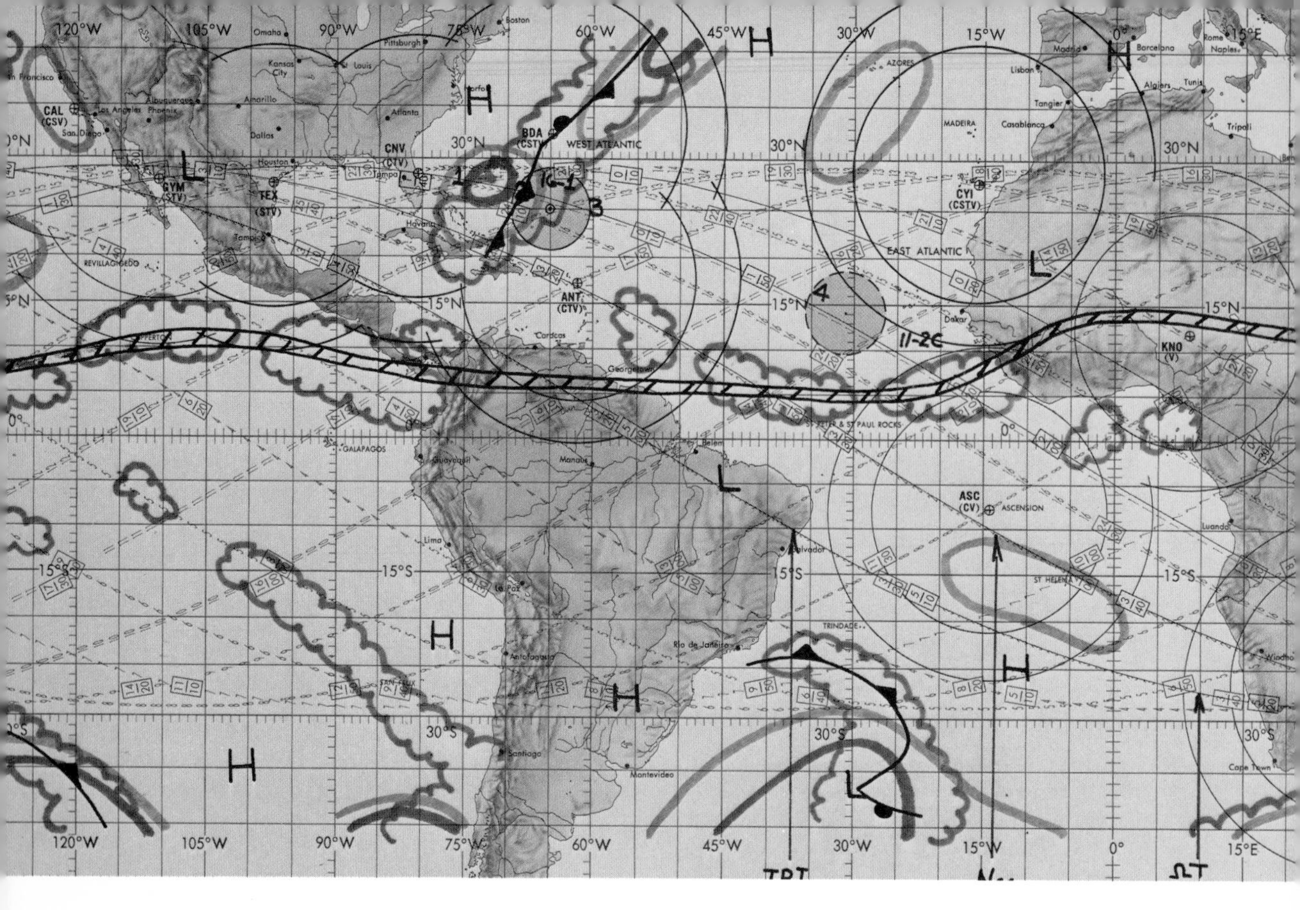

The breast-pocket sketch of weather around the globe was made by a weatherman for one of the Gemini astronauts. It shows the horizontal pattern into which the restless air was to form for a moment in time. The astronaut could tell at a glance where storm centers would be on the day of splashdown. Good places to stay away from!

Look up at the sky. The weather you see overhead this instant is part of a horizontal global pattern of cloudy skies and fair. This pattern has traveled thousands of miles horizontally about the globe to reach you. It will go on past you. The clouds above do not just appear, only to disappear when you no longer see them. Fair skies and clouds have their own past, present, and future—that is, what and where they have been, are now, and will be.

Tracking the horizontal flow of air about the earth is a large part of the weatherman's job. It was Benjamin Franklin who first observed the movement of weather pat-

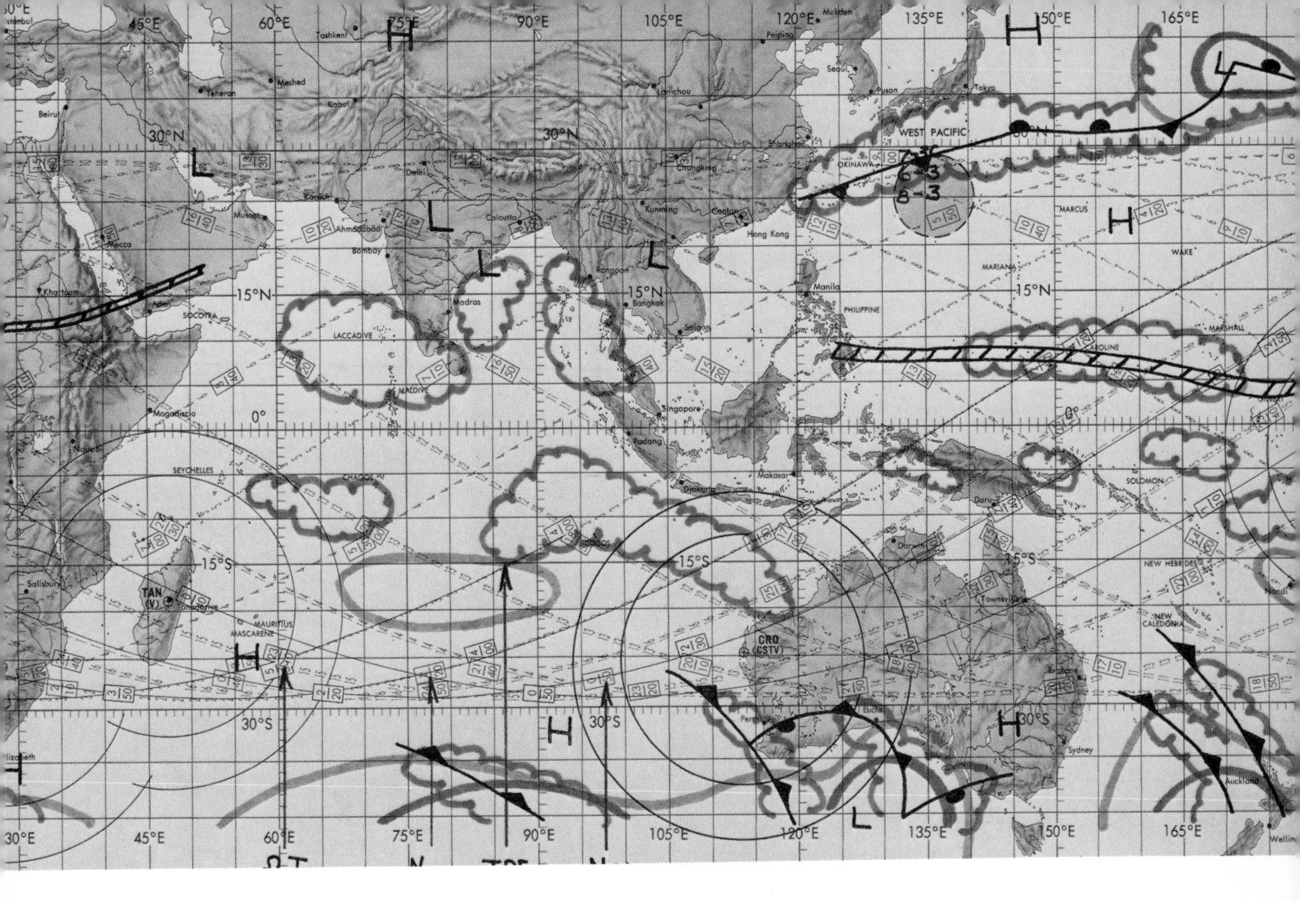

terns. In 1743 he wrote about his observation:

> . . . we were to have an eclipse of the moon at Philadelphia on Friday evening, about nine o'clock. I intended to observe it, but was prevented by a northwest storm, which came about seven . . . Yet when the post brought us a Boston newspaper . . . I found the beginning of the eclipse had been well observed there, though Boston lies NE of Philadelphia about 400 miles . . . I therefore mentioned it in a letter to my brother, who lived at Boston, and he informed me that the storm did not begin with them till near eleven o'clock . . . And upon comparing all other accounts I received from the several Colonies, of the time of beginning of the same storm, and since that of other storms . . . *I found the beginning always later the farther north-eastward* . . . I think . . . an hour every hundred miles.

Ben Franklin's weather sleuthing was later made into usable fact by other scientists. Maps were made, based

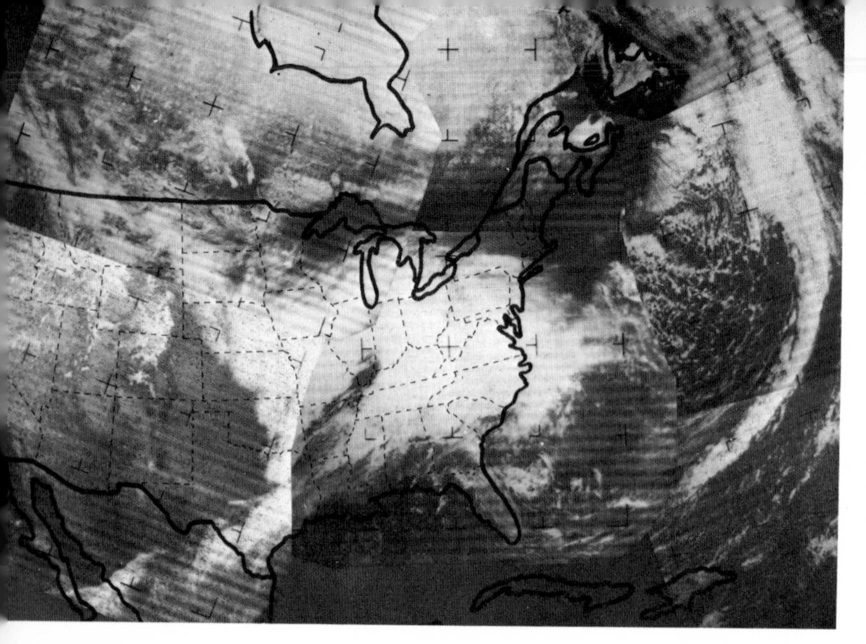
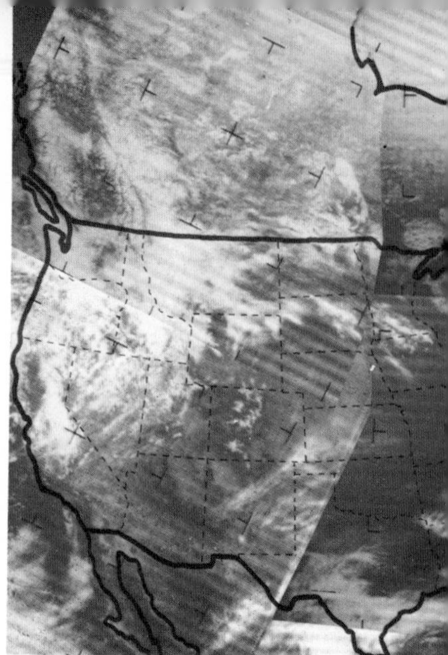

upon obsrvations at different stations around the world.

The tracking of this restlessness of air on a horizontal plane led to new findings. The United States Weather Bureau set up new stations. There are about three hundred in this country today.

As more information was accumulated, it became apparent that this movement of weather could be used as a basis for forecasting. In the middle latitudes of the earth, the forces that control weather move at predictable speeds along predictable paths. If you know the path and speed of something that moves, you can forecast where it will turn up next, and how soon it will get there.

The continental United States lies precisely in the middle latitudes of the Northern Hemisphere. Our weathermen took advantage of that fact, and learned to use the predictability of air flow here as a basis of forecasts.

Over the continental United States, the restless troposphere falls into patterns that travel horizontally from west to east. The speed of this air flow varies. In summer, patterns of fair weather and foul average 500 miles a day. In winter, with stronger prevailing winds, they speed up to average 700 miles a day.

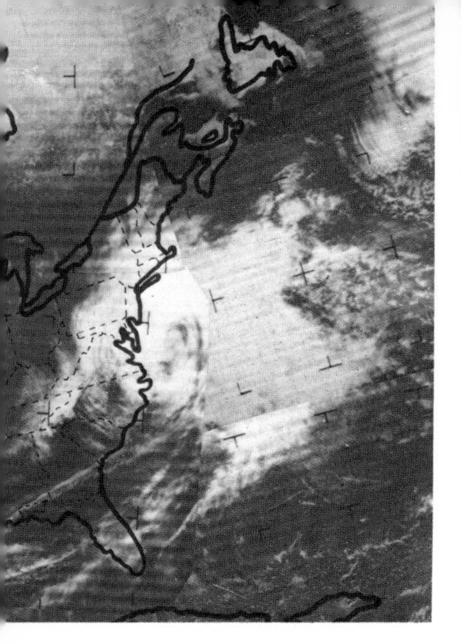

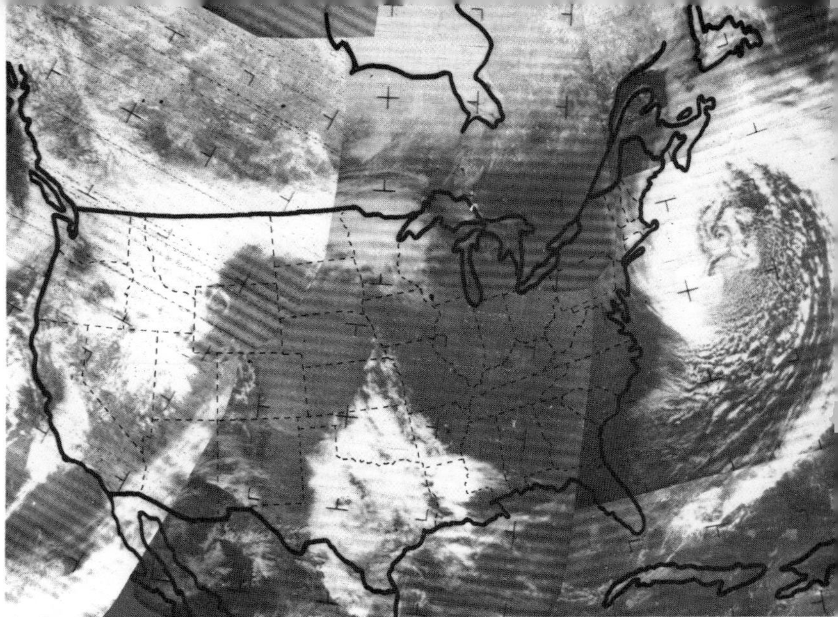

So far we have been tracking the horizontal flow of the restless troposphere about the earth. But weather, and the forces that create weather, also change vertically—upward into the skies. To "see" these vertical changes weathermen use some fascinating instrument-carrying devices. We will look at several in this book.

But horizontal or vertical, what are these weather-making forces? They are as invisible as air but the weatherman is trained to "see" them on his weather-measuring instruments. The weatherman watches his instruments most closely for changes in temperature, humidity, pressure, and winds.

Similar portable versions of station instruments used at every ground station are launched aloft to report vertical changes in the air above us. Measurements of these weather-changing forces are reported on the synoptic maps that show us conditions of weather across the country and the world.

Satellite photos of weather systems are overlaid by outline maps of the United States. Notice the horizontal movement of the storm center over the three-day period. Its path is from west to east—as the earth turns.

Instruments that measure temperature, pressure, humidity, and winds at progressively higher levels above the earth are put into several kinds of carriers. Airplanes and space satellites carry weather instruments. Instruments are also carried on ships and buoys to measure weather on the oceans. Of the airborne instrument carriers, the most common is the weather balloon. There are different kinds. Some are sent up without instruments, so that the weatherman can tell, by timing their ascent, the altitude of cloud ceilings over his station. The balloon we are going to launch will carry instruments. The instruments travel in a box called a RADIOSONDE.

The weatherman blows up a balloon with a gas lighter

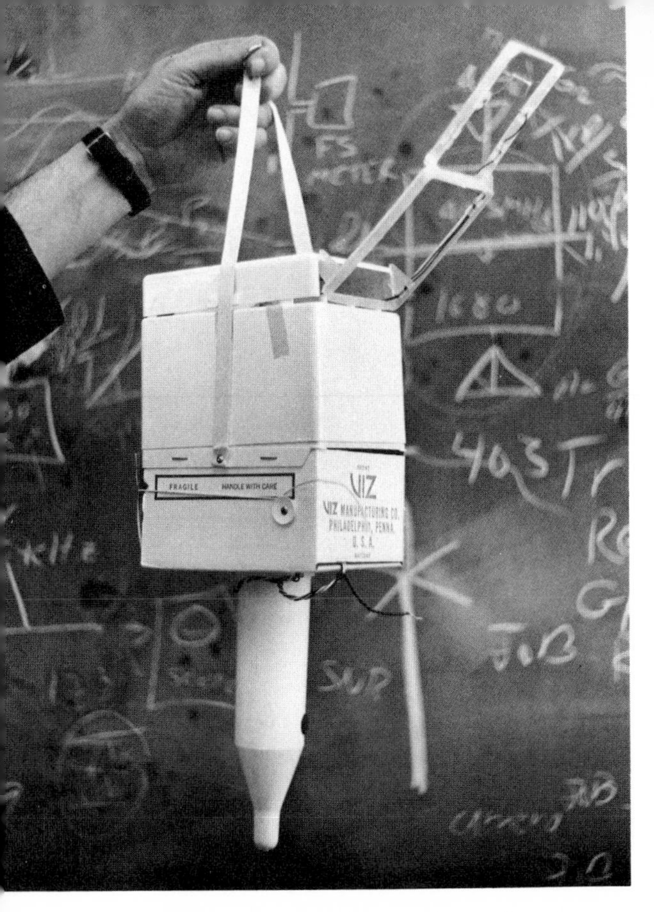

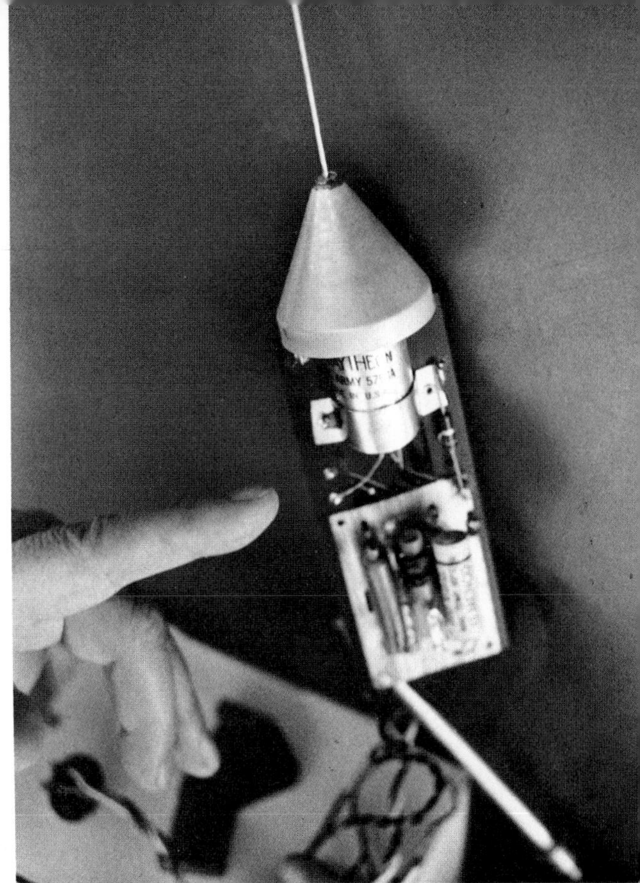

than air—usually helium. Six hundred thousand balloons sail the skies each year in the United States alone! The balloon will burst after it goes well into the stratosphere.

The box is called a radiosonde because it is equipped with a radio transmitter to "sound" or monitor the skies above. The radiosonde's transmitter sends signals to the station receiver set. These radio signals represent the numerical values of instrument measurements of temperature, humidity, and pressure. Let's look at the instruments contained in the radiosonde.

The instrument in the photograph, right, measures temperature. It is called a thermistor. It serves the same purpose as the station thermometer. This tiny ceramic needle travels outside the box, so as not to record the temperature of the radiosonde itself.

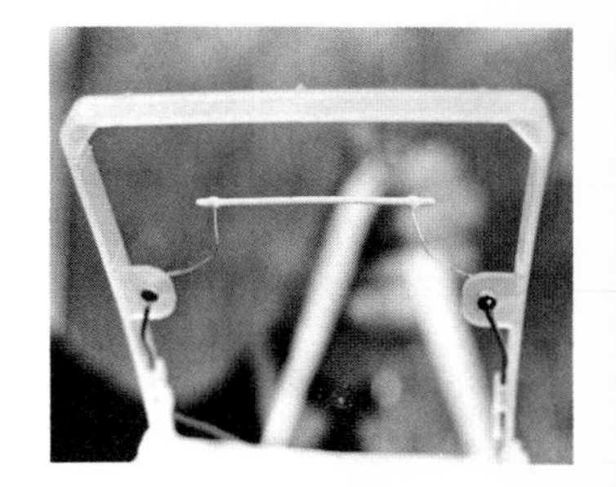

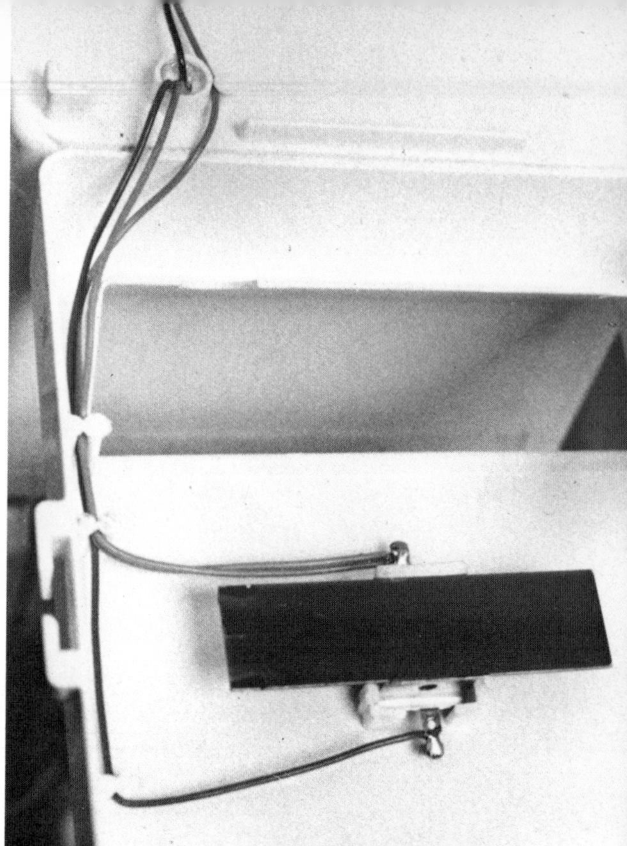

Air pressure registers on the instrument shown in the photograph on the left, above. The pressure gauge shows the weight of the air above the barometer on a calibrated scale. *Baro* is the Greek word for weight–a barometer is a weight-meter.

Humidity in air is measured by an element of carbon and its coil. At the station, humidity registers on psychrometers and hygrometers.

A postage-free mailing bag is tucked in so that anyone finding a grounded radiosonde will mail it back to the Weather Bureau. A radiosonde can be overhauled and sent aloft again. The balloon always bursts because the air inside the balloon meets less and less air outside at successively higher levels. It therefore expands until it bursts.

A kite is attached to the balloon to ease the radiosonde's fall–something like a parachute.

There she goes! This balloon was launched at Kennedy International Airport one fine April day. The weatherman launches two balloons daily in good weather, more when storms brew.

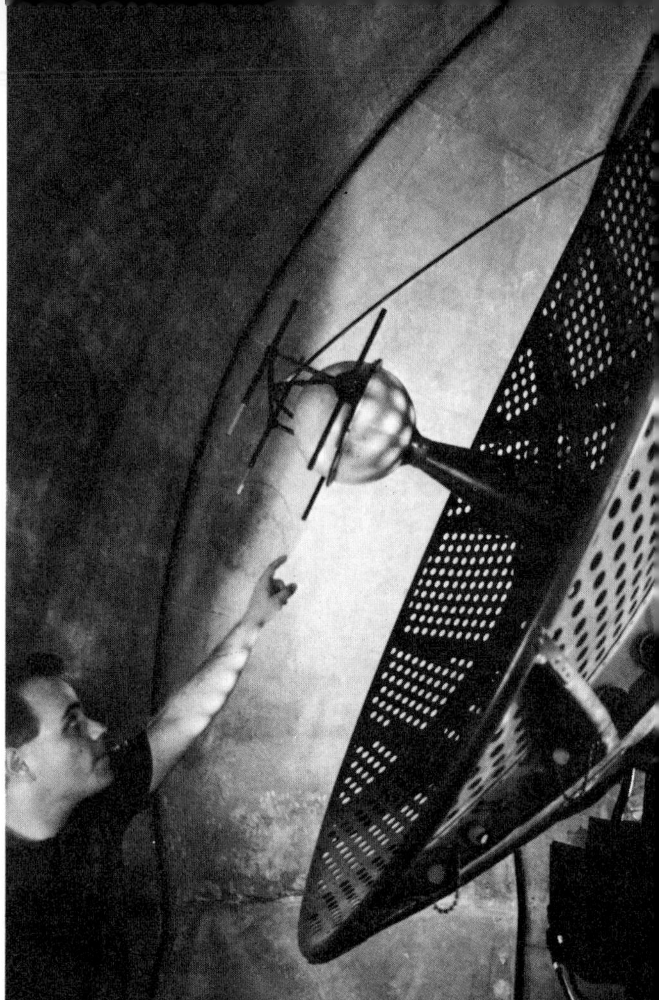

The weatherman rushes back to the station. Signals from the balloon's transmitter begin to come in almost immediately. They come to the dome-covered antenna shown in the photograph.

The antenna relays the signals to the station's receiver set. The signals form a continuing stream of data representing the numerical values of temperature, pressure, and humidity measured by the radiosonde's instruments. With charts, slide rule, and knowledge he has amassed from study and experience, the weatherman computes a report of the forces that are forming the weather aloft.

He types his report on a teletypewriter. Each key he presses registers on teletype receiver sets at other Weather Bureau stations on the circuit. One station on each circuit then relays the full report to the central station near Washington, D.C. If you have ever watched a teletype receiver, you know that when the message on it starts appearing, it seems as if it were being typed by a ghost. This report and others like it are links in the chain of data which forms the Weather Bureau's synoptic picture. A synoptic weather map is a map of a wide region compiled from observations taken in various places at or near the same time.

2. Forces Aloft

Temperature

If the earth heated the air above it to the same temperature all over the globe, there would be no weather change. The earth is not a smooth Ping-Pong ball. Oceans, forests, concrete-filled cities, deserts, green valleys, mountains—all these surfaces take in and radiate different intensities of heat.

All heat comes to earth from the earth's sun. The earth absorbs the sun's heat. It absorbs this heat in daytime only. But it loses heat by radiation both day and night.

Just as the sun radiates—sends out—its heat, so, to a much lesser degree, does the earth radiate warmth. But because of the differences in the rate of radiation and absorption from place to place, the sun-warmed earth is an uneven heater. Without these differences there would be no varieties in hotness or coolness from place to place. It would be no cooler in the shade of a tree, for example, than it would be in a barren field near the tree.

This phenomenon has an important effect on weather. It is the contrast in hotness and coolness of the air above the sun-warmed earth that creates all the things we know, feel, and see as weather.

Patches of unevenly heated air break away from gravity's grip, and go mixing, swirling, turning in the restless troposphere.

If it weren't for the sun-warmed earth's uneven heating, the air of the troposphere would move in orderly fashion with the earth as the earth rotates; that is, from west to east. Of course the movement, as Ben Franklin noted, is predominantly west-to-east. But these differences in temperature create slight differences in the paths and speeds of air masses. And when you consider the vastness of this globe we live on, you can see that even a slight variation is bound to affect the weather in and over your city.

Weathermen track this restlessness of the troposphere as best they can. One way is by recording the degree of hotness or coolness of the swirling air masses. This gives us a clue to the global weather patterns, and their influence on local weather.

Temperature-watching on a local level is important, too. It helps us lead more predictable lives–plan our business and our play. The march of temperatures over the years is an important statistic in helping weather scientists unravel many of the mysteries of the way weather behaves.

Perhaps the most recognized fact about weather is that prevailing temperatures are different in different parts of the earth. We have all heard of the cold poles, the hot equator. The belts in between are the temperate zones. It

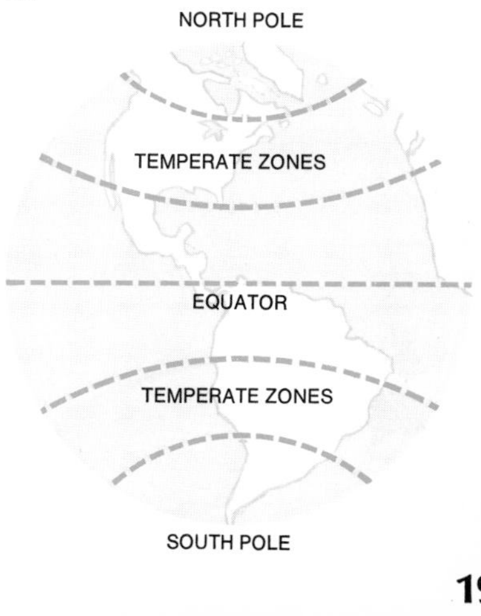

NORTH POLE
TEMPERATE ZONES
EQUATOR
TEMPERATE ZONES
SOUTH POLE

is here that weather changes are the most dramatic. We will explore the hows and whys of these divisions in future chapters.

Temperatures, then, vary horizontally about the earth. But they also vary with altitude. That is why the balloon-borne radiosonde carries a thermistor. It is the weatherman's job to track temperatures on a horizontal plane—from station to station. But it is also important to know its upward profile. These two perspectives tell a great deal about weather change.

If you were flying a light plane, you could get into the cockpit on a warm day, mop your brow, start off and climb into the skies. At an altitude of 8,000 feet you might be wishing for a sweater! Air is cooler the higher above the earth you take a temperature reading. That is because, as we have said, the sun-warmed earth is the air's source of heating. The farther from earth a parcel of air is found, the cooler it will be. This is only true in the troposphere, however. Beyond the swirling masses of air, temperatures begin to increase. That is because the sun heats the thin layers of air there more directly.

But in our region of turning, mixing, swirling air, temperatures decrease upward from earth. The rate of cooling is about 3.3 degrees Fahrenheit for every 1,000 feet of distance from earth.

If the weatherman knows that air temperature lapses upward at a standard rate, why is he sending the radiosonde's thermistor aloft?

The reason is that this standard rate of cooling is an average that applies to the troposphere as a whole. By comparing this reference point with findings for his part of the troposphere and with reported findings from nearby stations, the weatherman has a good clue to weather change. The findings at the station and at ever higher levels aloft give him a picture of air temperatures. If there is a significant contrast between temperatures aloft and those nearby, there will be weather action in the area.

Humidity

The moisture in air is called HUMIDITY. Air is made up of many different particles of matter. Most of these particles are in gas form. A gas is something you do not see. It is matter, nonetheless. One kind of invisible particle in the invisible veil of air that is all around us is water. Particles of water are made up of a "marriage" of two kinds of very important gases—oxygen and hydrogen. Water-in-air, moisture, or humidity, whichever you wish to call it, is a very important part of weather-making. It forms the aspect of weather you can see—the cloud.

Water can exist as a vapor, as a liquid, or as a solid. Let's see how this property of water figures in weather-making. We will make a kitchen cloud! First step is to boil some water. As the liquid water in the kettle heats up, it begins to escape into the air as a vapor. The process is called EVAPORATION. Similarly, the earth's radiant heat makes water evaporate into the sky. Odd as it may seem, the oceans do their own evaporating. They use warmth stored at lower levels to heat water at the surface.

Evaporating water is invisible—in our kitchen and in the sky. See the space between the kettle and the steam? That is invisible evaporated air. The steam "cloud" over our

kettle, and the clouds overhead, become visible by the process of CONDENSATION. When escaping water vapor meets cooler air, it will condense into a visible cloud of steam—over the kettle. Over the earth, water vapor particles are cooled by the expansion of rising air. The particles then condense around particles of impurity—to form visible fog or clouds.

Then, when the contrast in temperatures becomes sharper, and other factors come into play, the water-in-air returns to its liquid state—as PRECIPITATION. Rain is liquid precipitation. But precipitation can occur in the solid state —snow and hail.

It is surprising, because water-in-air is so big a part of weather, that there is really very little water vapor in air. Some places there is none. The air is dry. Usually there is no more than 4% of the total volume of air. But this little bit of moisture or humidity trapped by gravity in the troposphere can brew quite a tempest in the teapot of weather.

Hovering in an invisible, vapor state, it can make us quite uncomfortable. Or it can become visible as fog, clouds, drizzle, rain, sleet, snow, and hail.

When the weatherman measures the hidden, lurking water vapor in air, he is measuring humidity. "How thick and heavy is the air today," we sometimes say. What we mean is, "How humid it is." What we should say about humid air is, "How light and thin it is." Here's why.

The tiny, invisible particles of air have weight. Particles of water vapor have a certain weight, too. Particles of air weigh more than particles of water vapor. Therefore, when water vapor mixes with air, it lightens the air. The more moisture air contains, the thinner and lighter it is.

There is a limit, though, to the amount of water vapor that air can hold. This limit is set by the temperature of the air. At any given temperature, the air can hold a certain amount of water vapor. Any more water vapor, and condensation of clouds will begin. Precipitation may follow.

Relative humidity tells us, in percentages, how much humidity the air is holding at a certain time and place, in relation to how much it *can* hold at the existing temperature. A relative humidity of 100% means that the air is saturated; that is, filled to capacity with water vapor. It can hold no more. Condensation and precipitation appear.

Clouds often do form below this saturation point, however. A relative humidity as low as 80% is often enough to start cloud-making.

Dew point is the temperature at which a relative humidity of 100%–saturation–is reached. Dew, or liquid drops, appear.

Weathermen measure humidity in several ways. Besides the hygrometers and psychrometers at the station, the balloon we launched carried a humidity-measuring element aloft.

The capacity of air to hold water decreases by half for every 20 degrees Fahrenheit of cooling. Because the vapor escaping into the skies rises through ever cooler layers of air, humidity readings at many altitudes above the earth are an important part of the weatherman's report.

A cloud is defined as condensation hovering at least 50 feet above the earth. Below this level, visible moisture is called FOG or MIST. When it is full of impurities, it is called SMOG.

Clouds form when water evaporates off the earth and cools in the air above. The escaped water vapor particles become part of the mixture that is air. But water vapor may hover unseen indefinitely. What makes it condense into a cloud particle and amass into clouds we can see? One important factor is the AEROSOL. Aerosols are impurities in air—invisible bits of dust, smoke, pollen, or sea salt. Water vapor particles cluster around these particles to become visible cloud particles. At least a thousand vapor particles come together to form one small cloud particle.

If the right kind of aerosols are missing in the atmosphere, or if there are not enough of them, the moisture will not condense into clouds. Without this important ingredient, the humidity could reach over 100%, and clouds still would not condense.

We often compare the shape of a cloud to an animal cracker or face. But the shape of a cloud tells the weatherman how it was formed and what it is likely to do.

Clouds are the wind's traveling companions. The shape of a cloud depends to a great extent on the kind of wind or air flow it was formed in.

The cloud in the photograph on page 24 forms in the horizontal flow of air. This flow is quite stable, covering hundreds or thousands of miles about the earth. If you fly a plane through stable air you feel no bumps. Clouds formed in stable air are smooth. They are layers of cloud particles. Layer clouds are called STRATUS. Not all stratus clouds precipitate. When they do, it is usually a steady drizzle. NIMBUS is a word meaning rain. Rain-bearing stratus clouds are called NIMBOSTRATUS. Fog, haze, mist, smog are all stratus formations.

The kind of cloud you see in the photograph below is formed in the vertical motion of air. Caused by rapid heating and cooling, the relatively small up-and-down currents disturb the stability of horizontally flowing winds. Flying through unstable air is a bumpy ride at best. At worst, the plane can be torn apart. Clouds formed in this kind of disturbance shape up as heaps and billows of cloud particles. They are called CUMULUS. Our fair-weather friends in the sky are often this type. But beware the CUMULONIMBUS! Nimbostratus may rain all it likes, but the cumulonimbus is the home of the fiercest storms.

The type of cloud you see in the photograph above gets its shape from the temperature rather than from the kind of air flow it is formed in. CIRRUS clouds look like locks or curls or dapples. They form as ice crystals, because they form near the top of the troposphere at low temperatures. Stratus and cumulus clouds may be made of liquid particles or of ice crystals or of a mixture of both states of water. But cirrus clouds are thin films of ice crystals alone.

These crystal clouds never precipitate. At best, they help stratus and cumulus clouds to precipitate. They do this by chilling particles of these clouds that rise to the cirrus's lofty heights. Because they form so high, cirrus clouds herald the coming of weather action.

These are the three basic cloud types. But these three shapes combine to form enough variations to fill a lengthy and fascinating cloud atlas. Some of the combinations you may see aloft are stratocumulus, cirrostratus, and cirrocumulus. Usually, the clouds you see are a combination rather than a pure type.

Pressure

We now know a little about how heat affects air and water vapor. Now let's see how heat sets air in motion.

Air is matter. Matter has weight. Particles of air have weight, though not much weight, to be sure. Still, the total weight of the atmosphere is about six quadrillion tons! Not very "airy," is it?

The weight of air creates pressure, just as your body does when you press a hoe into the ground. Your weight exerts pressure on the hoe. So it is with air. Quite simply, air pressure presses. High pressure presses a lot. Low pressure presses little. Many air particles weigh more than few air particles do. Therefore, a large amount of air particles will create more pressure than a small amount.

Air particles are not evenly spaced in the atmosphere. Besides, they are always dancing about, changing places. In some places at some times there are many particles clustered together. At other times and places there are less.

Dense air occurs in a place and time when there are many air particles squeezing together and jogging about. This air is heavy air. It weighs much. It presses a lot.

Thin air occurs when and where there are few air particles. Thin air doesn't weigh as much as dense air. It is light. It is also weak–it cannot exert much pressure.

In other words, heavy, dense air exerts a greater air pressure than does light, thin air. The weatherman knows that air, like any gas or vapor, will act in certain predictable ways. Air always flows from an area where it is dense and high-pressured to invade the territory of thin lower-pressured air. If the weatherman knows where the air is dense and where it is thin, he can predict which way the air will be flowing.

Wind is no more–and no less–than air on the move. We can stir up a breeze by squeezing a lot of air into a balloon. The densely packed air in the balloon is a high-pressure area. The air around the balloon is thinner and lower-pressured. Holding the balloon in one hand, we release the nozzle. The dense air flows out of the balloon, invading the area of the lower-pressured, thinner air around. How do we know? It creates enough of a breeze to make the candle flame flicker.

Heat from the sun-warmed earth is one factor in creating and changing the density of air. Heating makes particles of air move fast, spreading and spacing them out. Cooling–the relative absence of heat–makes particles of air compress, or come together densely.

This ability of air to expand with heating and compress with cooling is the force that makes air move. If the earth heated the air evenly, masses of air would not break away from the neat rotational pattern to swirl about. As it is, they do escape, flowing from high pressure into low pressure.

It is the difference in density created by temperature contrasts that creates differences in air pressure. These, in turn, loosen gravity's grip on the air of the troposphere. Weathermen expect a HIGH where air is cool and therefore dense. Where air is warm and thin, they look for a low-pressure area—a LOW.

Simple? Not altogether. If low temperature meant high pressure and high temperature meant low pressure *all* of the time, the weatherman would have a much easier job than he does. Unfortunately for him, the *density* of air can change with a change within the pressure system itself. That is, regardless of temperature. How?

Just the way we blew up the balloon. We did not change the temperature much. We *added* pressure to existing pressure. So it is in the skies. If parcels of warm air pile up, pressure will increase, resulting in a *warm* high. If cold air is forced away by outside pressure, the result is a *cold* low.

That keeps the weatherman checking pressures and not relying on temperature alone. And pressure, like temperature, changes with altitude as well as horizontally about the earth.

For every 1,000 feet of altitude, air pressure drops by one inch of mercury, or 34 millibars on a barometer that is not based on the mercurial nature of mercury. Standard sea level pressure (at 59 degrees Fahrenheit) is 29.92 inches of mercury—or 1013.2 millibars. As with temperature, the upward decrease in pressure is due to less heating of and less gravitational pull on fewer particles of air encountered.

But if we know the standard rate of decrease, why send a pressure gauge up in the radiosonde? The weatherman is looking for very slight changes and differences which, when compared to this standard rate for the whole atmosphere, and to readings reported at other stations, will give him another powerful clue to weather change.

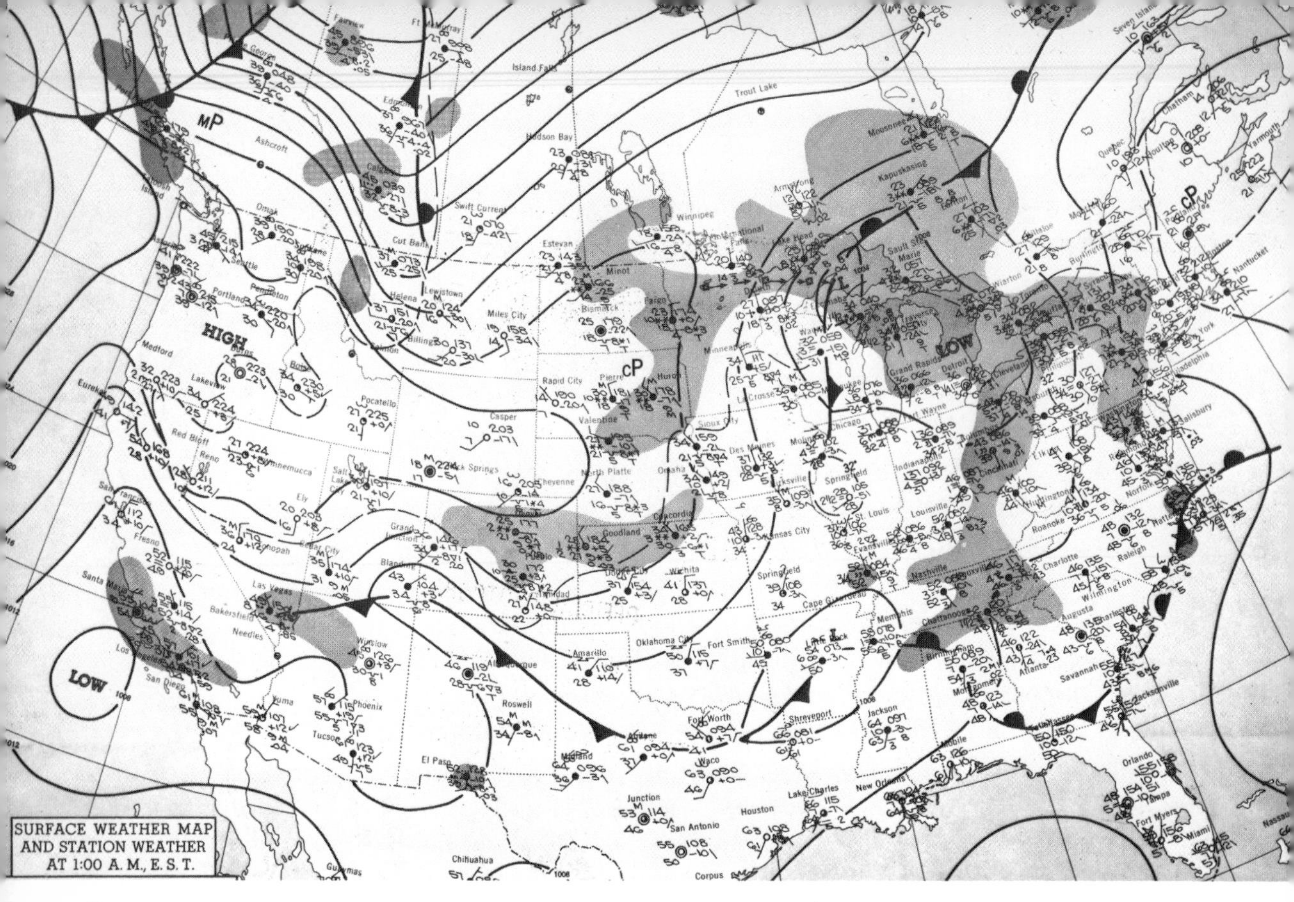

SURFACE WEATHER MAP AND STATION WEATHER AT 1:00 A.M., E.S.T.

With these reports, and with station readings all over the country, a weatherman at the Washington mapping station can chart the invisible forces that control air flow. He bases his nationwide forecasts on this. He plots his high and low patterns a bit like a game of connect-the-dots.

These lines in weather maps are called ISOBARS—lines of equal air pressure. The weatherman draws isobars by connecting dots of equal pressure reported by stations along a certain area. Each isobar is labeled in inches of mercury or in millibars.

If the dots of equal pressure connect into a free-form circle, the weatherman has tracked a pressure center. If the pressure here is higher than in areas around it, it is a high. Air will flow *outward* from this center, over several hundred to 2,000 miles. Good chance of fair weather here.

If the dots connect into a center of pressure lower than those around it, it is a low. Air will be moving *inward*, from high pressure areas around it. A low is small, but just watch the weather action!

High and low—they are invisible. We see them only by the clouds that shape up around them. But these unseen forces control winds, bring storms, create fair weather or precipitation. They are the American weatherman's most valuable aid in forecasting for the continental United States. They create the movement of storms which Ben Franklin observed.

Outside the middle latitudes of the earth, weathermen do not have the movement of highs and lows as a basis for forecasts. At the poles, cold, dense air heaps up in semipermanent highs. At the hot equator, warm, thin, light air forms semipermanent lows. But in the temperate middle latitudes, cold air moving away from the poles meets warm air moving away from the equator. Here the highs and lows are ever on the move.

3. Patterns of Weather

Winds

So far we have been identifying the basic forces that are behind what brews in the caldron of weather. Now let's look at the hows and whys of the phenomena these forces produce. Local weather conditions as well as nationwide patterns are really part of the global flow of air. First let's see just how air flows or circulates about the globe.

Once air is set in motion by differences in pressure, which in turn are created by the sun-warmed earth's uneven heating, the path it travels is guided by a force arising from the earth's own rotation. This is the CORIOLIS FORCE, named after the scientist who detected it.

The diagram on the left on page 33 shows how air would circulate about the earth if the earth stood still. There would be no Coriolis force to deflect winds and set them in the global patterns we know.

To understand this diagram, let's go back to the way a vapor such as gas is known to behave. When a gas is heated, its particles will expand and *rise*. When a gas is cooled, its particles will compress and *sink*. Air heated at

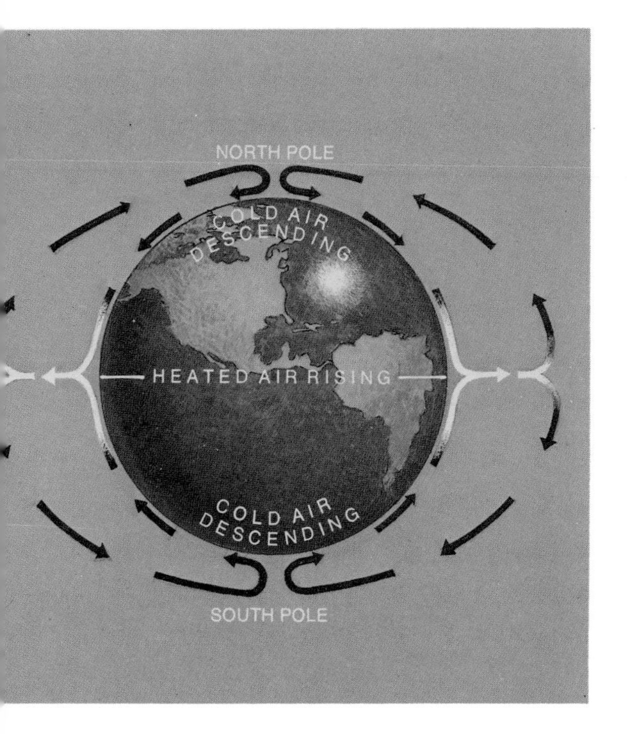

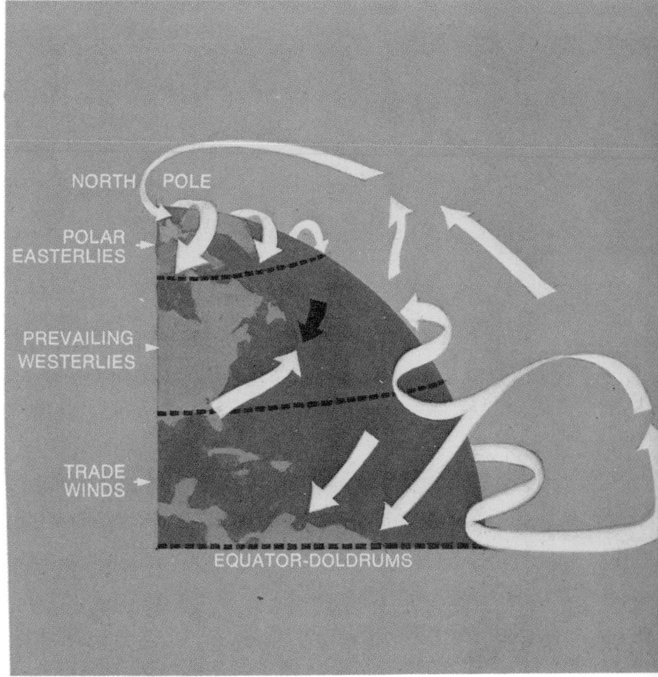

the equator rises, while air cooled at the poles sinks. The sinking, heavy air chases the light, thin air in this simple pattern.

But because the earth does *not* stand still, the neat general circulation shown in the diagram is affected by the movement. Air does rise and sink as described. But its paths are not that perfect as seen in the diagram on the right. Arising out of the earth's rotation, the Coriolis force works on the flow. It deflects the paths of winds–and of any free-moving object about the earth.

In the Northern Hemisphere, winds travel a little to the *right* off course. In the Southern Hemisphere, winds deflect a little to the *left*.

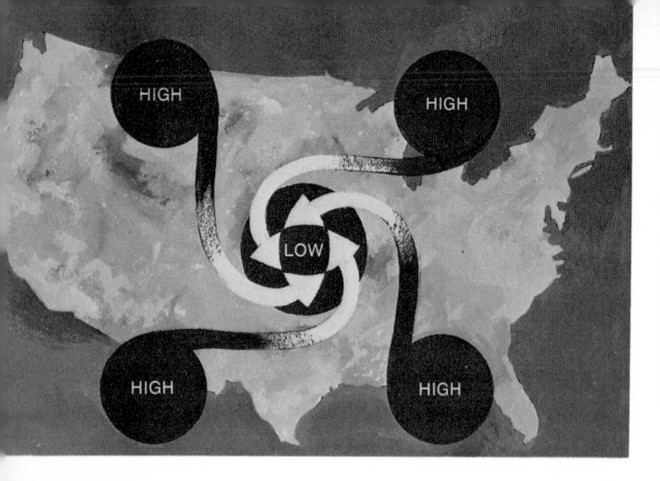

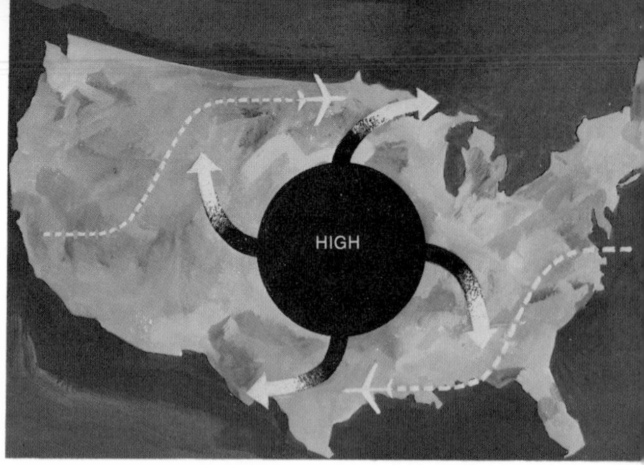

Because of the deflections, the Coriolis force sets the path of prevailing winds. The United States is under the influence of the prevailing westerlies. The westerlies overlie local winds and breezes. Local winds are the work of smaller-scale patterns of heating and cooling that result in pressure change.

Because of the Coriolis effect, air flows *clockwise* out of a high. It flows *counterclockwise* into a low. In the Northern Hemisphere, that is. The reverse is true in the southern half of the globe. Now that is a valuable thing for the weatherman to know. He uses it to predict the direction of wind flow about a pressure center.

At the top of the troposphere and around it flows a wave-like river of strong air currents. It is called the JET STREAM. Wind speeds here are up to 300 miles per hour, though 150 miles per hour is most common. Weather scientists are still trying to determine the jet stream's role in weather-making. They know that it overlies the seasonal flow of prevailing winds, and reflects (or is reflected by) that season's prevailing winds. This is particularly so in the temperate zones (the middle latitudes) of the earth. The jet stream girdles the hemisphere.

In the Northern Hemisphere, the jet stream overlies the prevailing westerlies, just as the prevailing westerlies overlie local winds and breezes.

Wind direction shows up on the wind vane. The arrow shows the direction from which, in reference to true north, the wind is blowing. A similar vane shows wind shifts. The vane transmits its reports by electric signals to the station receiver.

The cup anemometer shows the speed of winds. The rate at which the wind sets the cups spinning tells us wind speed and, on a similar anemometer, gustiness.

These instruments measure local winds and breezes. They also measure the prevailing westerlies, indirectly, because local winds are influenced by prevailing winds.

Weather maps show wind direction by the tilt of the wind symbols. The feathers and flags on the symbols show the speed.

DIRECTION OF WIND

WEST WIND EAST WIND

WIND SCALE miles per hour	CALM	1-4	5-8	9-14	15-20	21-25	26-31	32-37	38-43	44-49	50-54	55-60	61-66	67-71	72-77

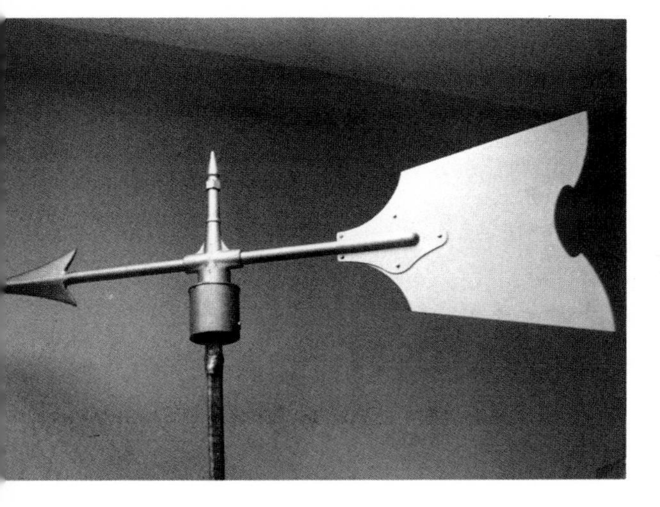

Air Masses

We in the continental United States live in the battle zone of air masses. In these temperate latitudes of the Northern Hemisphere (and in their mirror-image in the Southern), there is always change aloft. The temperate zones are the meeting place of cold air moving away from the poles and warm air moving away from the tropics; that is, the areas around the equator.

Where cold air meets warm air, a battle zone develops. This battle zone is called the POLAR FRONT. It girdles the whole hemisphere in a wavy band of weather action.

The boundary of the white zone is the polar front.

Air hovering for days, unchanging, over the poles or the equator, takes on the temperature and humidity of its source region. The weatherman then calls it an AIR MASS. An air mass is a body of air with the same temperature, moisture, and density measuring over 1,000 miles, horizontally. It measures about three miles on the vertical plane.

A slight pressure change at the source will set an air mass traveling. Weathermen identify each traveler by its source, its temperature in relation to that of the surface over which it moves, and by its speed and degree of stability. Its moisture depends on whether it is MARITIME (formed over oceans) or CONTINENTAL (formed over land).

Polar air masses are cold and travel to the southeast. They sink to the earth's surface because they are dense and heavy.

Tropical air masses move up from tropical regions. They rise, being thin and light. Slowly they move in a northeasterly direction.

Masses formed over oceans are usually moist. Masses formed over land are usually dry. The United States' winter weather is mostly the work of the frisky, dry polar air masses battling the warm, moist tropical foes.

When two air masses move toward each other and meet, they do not usually mix and mingle. They are kept separate by their different temperatures, densities, and moisture contents. A sloping battle zone is set up at the inner boundary of the meeting masses. It is called a FRONT.

The front is a broken part of the wavy polar front that girdles the hemisphere. It can be narrow—two or three miles—or it can be up to 70 miles wide at the ground. Wide or narrow, it is along this zone that weather action will develop.

In the diagram below, a warm air mass overtakes cold, slides up over the sunken wedge of cold air. Eastbound clouds: heralding cirrus announce the front because they are the highest. They indicate that moisture has been lifted and ice crystals are condensing.

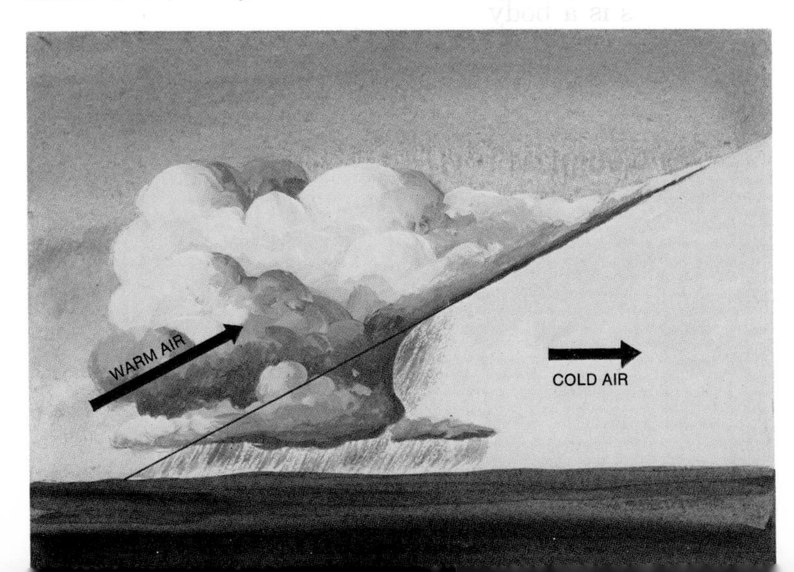

Expect rain or snow 24 to 36 hours after you spot these clues of moisture-lifting. Then the sky cover lowers, in a steady procession of cirrostratus, altostratus, and nimbostratus. Rain!

Southeasterly winds and a drop in pressure alert the weatherman to the slow arrival of a warm front. As it passes your city, winds shift to the southwest, the barometer shows a rise in pressure; the temperature, too, is up. Precipitation stops and the sky clears.

In the diagram below, cold air is overtaking warm air mass, tossing the warm air aloft by wedging under it. The action comes fast as a rule. Precipitation occurs from 12 to 30 hours after the heralding cirrus are seen. These high ice crystal clouds often form the anvil-shaped tops of thundering cumulonimbus. Cumulonimbus clouds descend with a cold front after cirrostratus, altostratus, or altocumulus clouds have paraded swiftly by. Thunderstorms in summer are the result. In winter, heavy rains, snow, sleet, hail can occur.

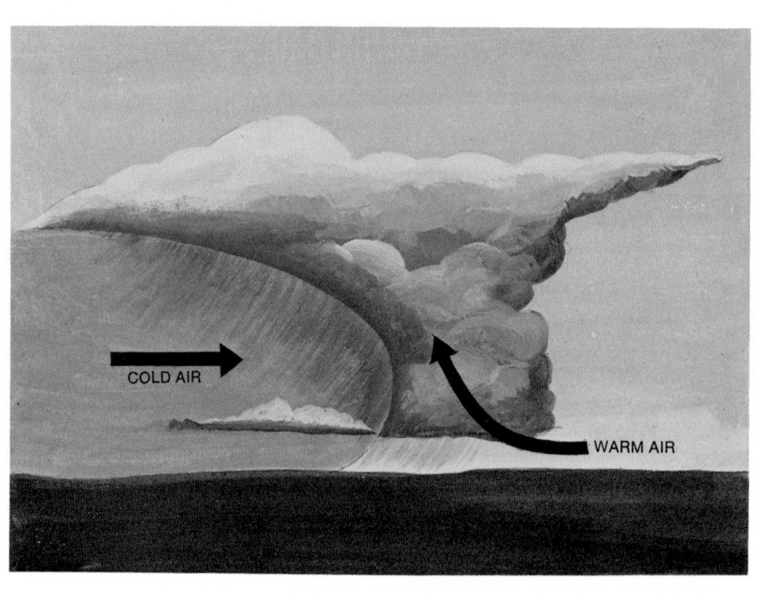

Winds from a southwesterly direction and a sharp drop in pressure tell of an approaching cold front. When it passes, due east, winds shift to the north and northwest. Pressure rises and temperature drops as the victorious cold air moves on.

A line of thunderstorms caused by gusting winds, called SQUALLS, often forms in advance of an active cold front. A SQUALL LINE looks something like the cloud formation in this photo. Squall lines form because warm, moist air precedes the cold front, and the atmosphere becomes unstable. This instability creates the gusting winds and these precoldfrontal storms. A squall line is a narrow band of weather activity—only fifty to a hundred miles across. But it can span the whole United States!

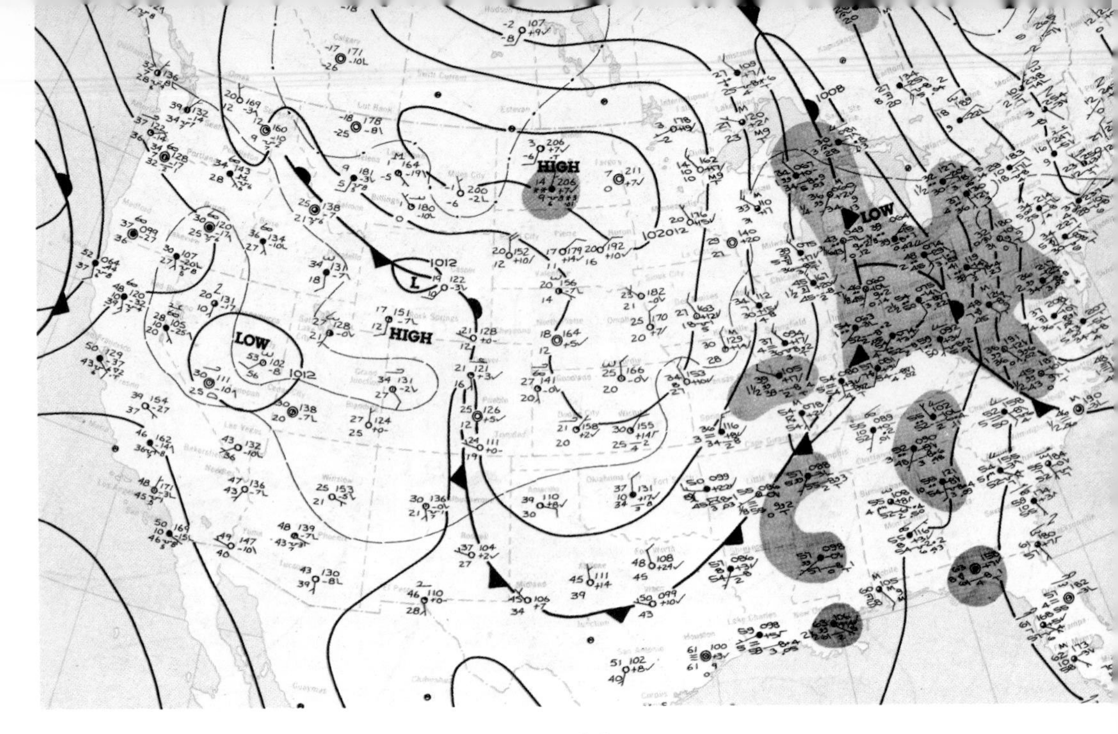

A warm air mass trapped between two cold air masses is called an OCCLUDED FRONT. These air masses force the warm air higher and higher. Expect warm front characteristics, followed by those of a cold front. An occlusion can last three or four days.

These weather maps show the flow of highs and lows, of fronts and precipitation over two days. The shaded areas show precipitation. Notice that the general movement is in an easterly direction.

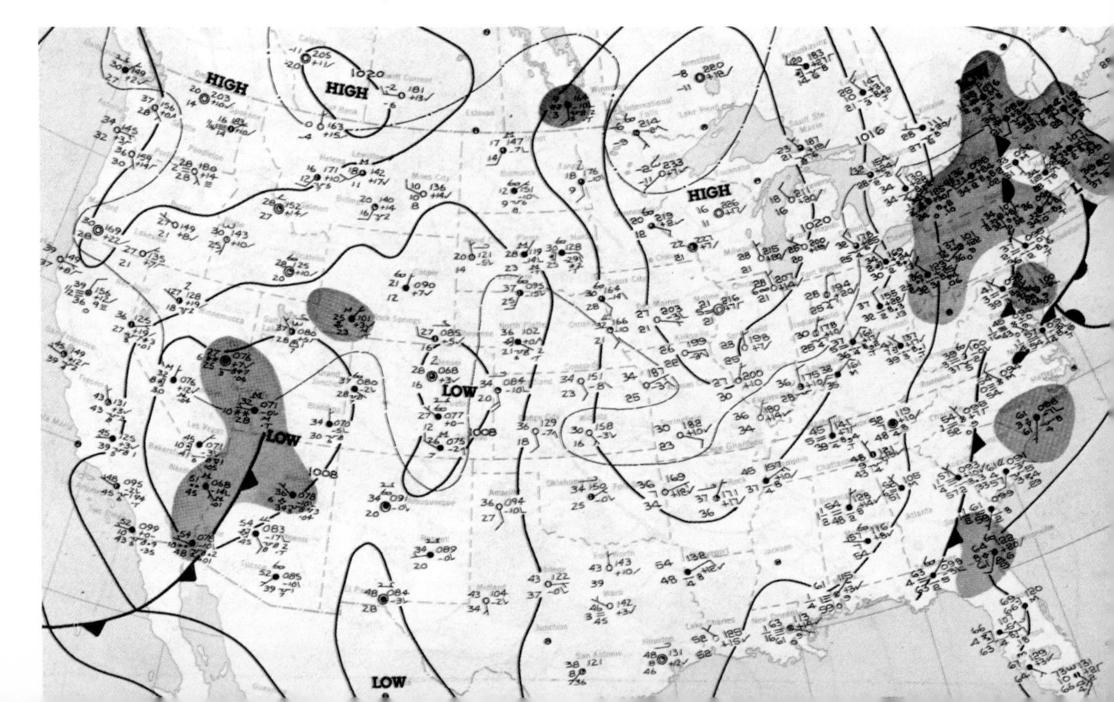

Clouds

After all this talk about weather action, let's look at some of the products of moving air and its accompanying clouds.

A thousand water vapor particles cluster around an aerosol to form one cloud particle. Ten million cloud particles cluster to form one raindrop. But how and when does this happen? Weathermen believe that different kinds of rain formation are at work under differing circumstances.

Rain forms when warm air meets cold air. Then water vapor cools, condenses around aerosols, and sometimes precipitates when the cloud particles, in their turn, cluster around aerosols.

The clustering of cloud particles to form a raindrop happens in several ways. When cold particles approach warmer ones, they steal the moisture from the warmer ones and grow in size until they are heavy enough to fall out of the cloud. When large cloud particles meet small ones, they grow at the expense of the small particles. When particles fall through a cloud, responding to the pull of gravity, they grow by picking up particles from layers through which they fall.

Super-cooled water droplets are particles that remain liquid at below-freezing temperatures because the aerosols are not right for the formation of ice crystals. When these water droplets are jogged up and down in unstable air, they evaporate on downdrafts and then cluster around crystals on updrafts. In each of these cases all that has happened is that the particles have grown large and heavy enough to fall out of a cloud.

Electrical attraction is another explanation weathermen give for rain formation. The study of atmospheric electricity is one of the newer concerns of meteorology—the science of weather. Yet the relation between atmospheric electricity and weather phenomena goes back to—you guessed it—Ben Franklin. It was he who first noted the presence of electricity in the atmosphere.

Electricity is a form of energy. Like heat energy, it is a mover and a changer of matter. In fact, one of its roles is to hold matter together, to bind atom to atom—the smallest particle of one kind of matter to another smallest particle of the same kind of matter.

Particles of all matter have the ability to take on an electrical charge. There are two kinds of electrical charges: POSITIVE (+ plus) and NEGATIVE (— minus). All we really need to know is that like charges repel each other, while unlike charges attract each other. The attraction of opposite charges on particles of matter is the "glue" which holds matter together.

Let's make some rain by electrical attraction. A meteorologist rubs two plastic disks together. This makes their electric charges separate. The minus charges group on the bottom disk. The plus charges migrate to the upper disk.

When the two disks are pulled apart, an electric field exists between them. An electric field is the possible path of influence between the two electric charges.

A spray of fine water droplets is directed between the two disks. Make believe they are cloud droplets. These droplets carry like charges—which is why they repel each other, and are separate droplets. (They may also be uncharged—neutral.)

The droplets pass before our newly generated electric field. Some take on a plus (+) charge. Others take on a minus (—) charge. Plus and minus do-si-do, finding attractive partners in the everlasting dance of electrically charged matter. Plus attracts minus. Tiny droplets come together to form large drops. Rain!

Rain is just one form of precipitation. *Drizzle*—the steady fall of tiny droplets from stratus clouds—is another. *Snow* is ice crystals clustered into flakes. Snow forms in the ups and downs of unstable air in any precipitating cloud. It is thought that the different shapes of snow depend on the chemical composition of air and water-in-air at the time of formation. *Hail* is solid pebbles of ice. In violent cumulonimbus clouds, accompanied by thunder and lightning, hailstones form from sleet and snowflakes. They cool on updrafts, melt on down drafts, pick up particles and collide with others, then freeze together.

Thunderstorm Brewing

Ben Franklin once decided to prove that lightning is the result of electricity present in the atmosphere during a thunderstorm. He did so. He stole some of this electricity from a thundercloud. Guiding it down from a high-flying kite, along the kite's cord to a metal key, Ben found that he could draw electric charges from the key. It was a dangerous thing to do. He might have electrocuted himself, but it turned out to be a very valuable experiment.

Weathermen all over the world tested Ben's findings.

They confirmed that indeed there *is* electricity in the atmosphere. At all times, not just during thunderstorms.

There is a steady flow of electricity between the earth and the upper atmosphere. This flow is more intense during a thunderstorm. The earth is the minus-charged "goal" of the electric field. The IONOSPHERE or ELECTROSPHERE, as it is called, is the electrically charged region of the atmosphere. A predominantly plus-charged "goal" of the electric field exists between the earth and the upper atmosphere.

Electricity always flows from the negative (—) end of an electric field to the positive (+) end. This means that there is a constant flow of minus charges escaping from earth, attracted to the plus charges of the electrosphere. In other words, the earth is constantly losing its electric charge. How does the earth get back its lost charges? Forty-four thousand thunderstorms rage over the earth each day, feeding electric charges back to earth.

Weather scientists have tested the electric charges of falling rain, snow, and hail. It turns out that these are usually plus-charged as they fall. It would seem, then, that they too have a job to do in balancing the atmosphere's electric budget.

Many people think that lightning is atmospheric electricity. It is not. This most spectacular part of a thunderstorm is but a giant spark produced by the separation of electric charges in a cloud. It is just an effect–and a dramatic one, at that–of electricity.

The separation of electric charges that leads to lightning can be compared to the electric field that was created by rubbing two disks together. The instability of a cumulonimbus cloud results in the lumping of large amounts of plus- and minus-charged particles in the cloud. These tend to group in opposite parts of the cloud. In other words, the cloud becomes an electric field.

When a large enough charge has collected in the thundercloud, a discharge flashes between the minus-charged and the plus-charged parts. This discharge is what we see as lightning. Lightning can also flash between two clouds, which act as opposing "goals" of an electric field, or between a cloud and the ground. The path that lightning takes depends on the distribution of electric charges at the time and place.

Most discharges never touch the ground. Lightning laces through thunderclouds and disappears. When it does touch down, however, it can explode brick or wood and cause great damage. Lightning retraces its path back to its cloud in a leaping up-stroke.

What makes a thunderstorm brew? Strong winds and very moist air. The winds provide the instability needed to lift the moist air very fast. The rapid lifting of moist air results in its rapid cooling. And the cooling of moisture releases a kind of energy called the LATENT HEAT of condensation. It is this released heat that powers the thunderstorm.

The rapid lifting of moist air can occur in several ways: by a frontal battle between a cold air mass and a warm air mass, by gusting winds ahead of a low, or by sudden heating from the earth's surface. This last way is how "lone wolf" thunderstorms form within a single air mass over warm land in summer. That is why they dissipate at twilight, as the earth cools. By and large, thunderstorms are the work of air mass contrast.

Let's see how a thunderhead works. We start with unstable air. Strong up-and-down currents build up a cumulus cloud. The cumulus works itself into a cumulonimbus in about an hour. Electric charges separate and group in opposite parts of the cloud. Soon there will be lightning and the accompanying sound, thunder. Precipitation, too, grows on the up-and-downdrafts. The wispy clouds at the top are cirrus–ice crystal clouds. They ice the cumulus cloud's particles. To the trained eye, they give the cumulonimbus cloud's intention. Each cumulonimbus cloud thunders for only about twenty minutes. But they usually work in teams, so that, as each "explodes," we think of the series as one continuous thunderstorm.

More rare than a thunderstorm—but not rare enough—is the weather demon known as a TORNADO, cyclone, or twister. Usually a tornado is formed by air mass contrast. But this is not always so. Because conditions that nurture a tornado are so similar to those that create an ordinary thunderstorm, weathermen have not yet accurately pinpointed the mechanism of this vicious whirlwind that descends suddenly to destroy all it touches. They have been able to refine their observations so that now the Weather Bureau can issue tornado warnings whenever there is a chance that this disaster may occur.

The only certain condition under which a tornado forms is the presence of a great deal of warm, moist air. On very hot, humid afternoons in late spring or summer, a tornado is possible almost anywhere. It most often descends on our central plains states.

The laboratory tornado is upside-down and tiny, but it is powerful enough to lift paper. Air currents are fed into the model box. As steaming water vapor, which represents the humidity in air, begins to rise, "clouds" begin to condense and spin in the air current to form the funnel that is our man-made twister.

In real life a violently spinning funnel of clouds forms around a center of very low pressure—a low. Wind speeds go up to 200 miles per hour. No more than 1,000 feet across, a tornado moves southwest to northeast at ten to fifty miles per hour. It reaches down like a finger out of its cumulonimbus home, and destroys. Then, like the lightning that accompanies it, the tornado retraces its path back to the cloud that brought it. In its wake, this savagely nimble low with its attendant winds and clouds, leaves a toll of lives and property. Thunder, rain, and hail are the tornado's sorry companions.

Hurricane Country

Outside the temperate latitudes, weathermen do not use the movement of fronts and pressure systems in forecasting. The reason is that weather changes here build up within single, semipermanent air masses, rather than by air mass contrast.

Where air masses do not battle, the seasons, too, are different. The arctic, for instance, does not warm up above 50 degrees Fahrenheit in summer. The tropics, that lush area about the equator, show wet and dry seasons rather than cool and warm ones. There is no movement of fronts outside the middle latitudes. Therefore, air pressure is not as important an indicator as it is in the United States.

Only about ten per cent of the earth's surface is monitored by weather instruments. The tropics, whose warmth starts the global circulation, still await their Franklin to unlock the patterns here. This area is still quite a mystery to the weatherman.

The DOLDRUMS—light, variable winds and calms—are the tropics' contribution to the global wind patterns. Nothing exciting ever happens here. Nothing, that is, but an occasional hurricane brewing. That, however, is more than enough drama and destruction to shake the "doldrums."

A HURRICANE is a severe storm with high winds cycling inward around a moving low. This in itself makes the hurricane an oddity. It is a moving low born where lows are usually unmoving. The low is the calm clear EYE in the center of the hurricane. Clouds whirl about the eye, carried on winds at speeds of 64 to 150 miles per hour. A rain shield forms on the edge.

Hurricanes feed on warm moist air above an ocean, developing in a single air mass, rather than by air mass contrast. Once hatched, the hurricane zigzags away from the

equator at a traveling speed of about 15 miles per hour. It covers 500 to 300,000 square miles.

The whirling is counterclockwise if the hurricane is north of the equator, like those that hit our Atlantic coast. South of the equator, the cycling is clockwise. In other words, it behaves like other lows in this respect. The Coriolis force, which is responsible for the deflection of winds, does not usually have an effect on the doldrums, which are the hurricane's parent winds. But when the sun moves north in summer, the doldrums follow the sun. Then these light, variable winds come into the areas within the scope of the Coriolis force. This encounter sets them cycling as hurricanes.

When summer comes to the North Atlantic, our eastern shores get a surge of hurricanes. In its summer, the South Pacific gets them. The North Pacific gets severe cyclonic storms like hurricanes. They are called TYPHOONS.

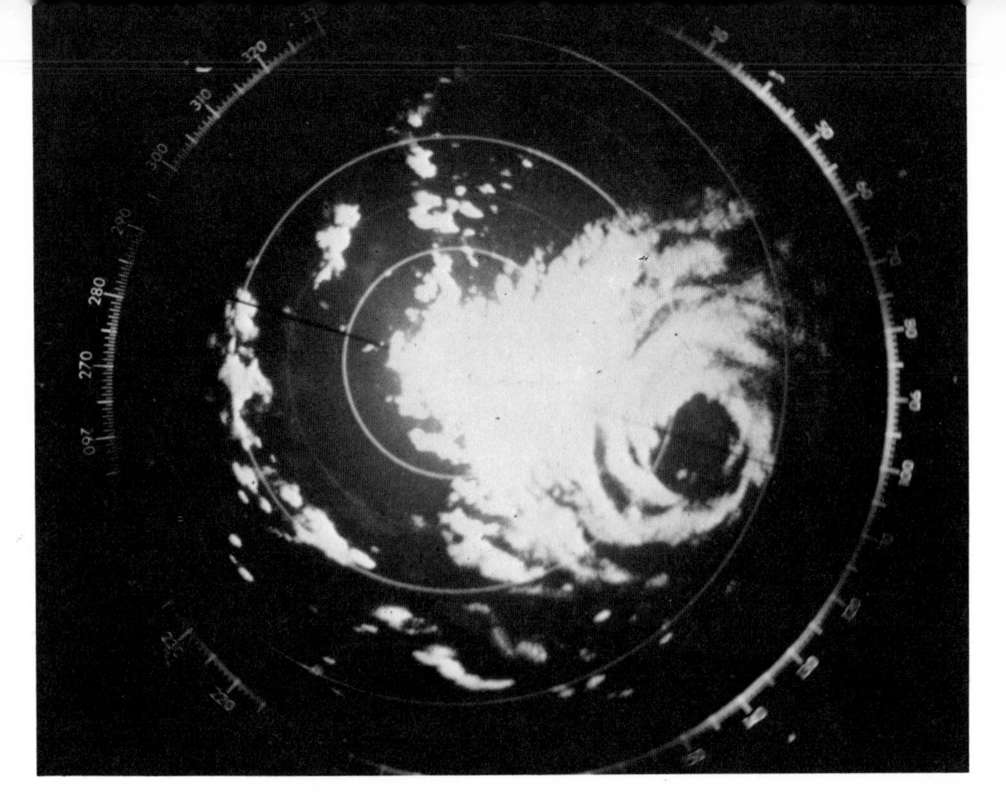

Radar beams bounce off precipitation in a 250-mile radius around a tracking station. They pick up hurricane and other storm patterns, which show up as signals, picked up by an antenna, which relays them to receivers and decoders. These transmit the signals onto a video screen. The radar beams show intensity as well as location of the precipitation. It wasn't until weathermen began to use radar to track hurricanes that they learned about the spiral-band structure.

4. Man's Control of Weather

Rain, Rain Go Away

Man has always tried to better his life by attempting to control the weather. Today weathermen are taking small, careful scientific steps to harness the powers of weather and turn them to man's use.

Cloud seeding is one way of grasping the reins of rainmaking away from a cloud. Dry ice or silver iodide, crystals like ice, are dropped from planes into fair-weather cumulus clouds. A few crystals can make the cloud precipitate!

Hurricane seeding is another control weathermen handle as carefully as one porcupine greets another. If you seed a hurricane over an ocean, you may steal its thunder. But what course will it take? You may just be rerouting it, perhaps adding to its violence.

Clouds about to pelt a crop with hail can be seeded to reduce the size of the stones or to make rain instead.

Weathermen are experimenting with these new techniques to cause changes in weather. But they are working very cautiously. Tampering with nature is a very dangerous undertaking. Every minute part of nature seems to

have its niche in the whole scheme of things, and changing one tiny factor can set off a chain reaction of changes. Some would not be desirable.

But the weatherman's greatest worry is that mankind in our century is causing the greatest changes in the atmosphere without concern for their aftereffects. We call this problem AIR POLLUTION.

Bits of smoke from natural forest fires have always been the aerosols in weather-making. So have bits of dust, sea salt, and pollen. They are the centers around which water vapor particles cluster to form cloud and precipitation particles.

But these smokestacks, too, send man-made smoke aerosols into the air. The world has never seen as much fuel-burning equipment as our century has produced.

Weathermen fear that these new aerosols will eventually block the sun's heat from coming to earth. Some of these aerosols react to the sun's ultraviolet radiation. This produces a complex chain reaction of chemical changes in the content of the air which harm man and his environment. Weathermen fear droughts as a result of air pollution. The chemistry of the air is an intricate balance. Throwing off the balance of anything in nature is a potential hazard. As we have seen, every tiny bit of weather-making is related to every other bit. So it is with the total scheme of nature. Man cannot tamper or pollute one part of nature without upsetting the applecart in other directions as well.

As it is, air pollution submerges our cities under almost unmoving clouds of unhealthy airborne pollutants. When a layer of air close to earth is trapped by an overlying layer of warmer air, it cannot rise. This is called a TEMPERATURE INVERSION. During temperature inversions, the pollutants are trapped over the city. At these times, the death toll rises.

Pollution is one good reason for seeking more complete answers to the mysteries of weather. There are several ways of finding out about the relation between the sun, the earth, air, water and aerosols.

One is by perfecting a mathematical model of the atmosphere; that is, by making a number-picture of complex equations.

To do this enormous job, the Weather Bureau station in Washington, D.C., has the largest compound of weather-calculating electronic computers in the world. A computer is a combination of equipment that takes in, selects, calculates and puts out information. It can calculate in split seconds what would take a mathematician weeks to work out on his slide rule.

Weathermen "feed" mathematical formulas for the known workings of weather, and the variables and unknowns coming in from station reports, into computers. Little by little, an ever more perfect mathematical picture of the atmosphere is emerging. Weathermen use these computers to work out long-range forecasts as well. A forecast for up to a two-week period may soon be commonplace.

Still, man does not yet have enough uses for his brainchild. This is true in all fields. A computer can only solve

problems based on questions that man asks it, and man is not supplying questions that tax the mechanical brain enough. Knowing what question to ask a computer is the most important part of solving a problem.

The weatherman must decide how he wants the information to be returned to him. And that depends on what he intends to do with it. He may want to chart some pressure systems, or map a nationwide forecast, or work on the mathematical model.

Computer tabulations can end up on punch cards for storage and statistics, on the teletype hookup for immediate use in forecasts, on paper and magnetic tape, in photo facsimile, as sound signals on a telephone that monitors the computer, or as visual signals on video screens.

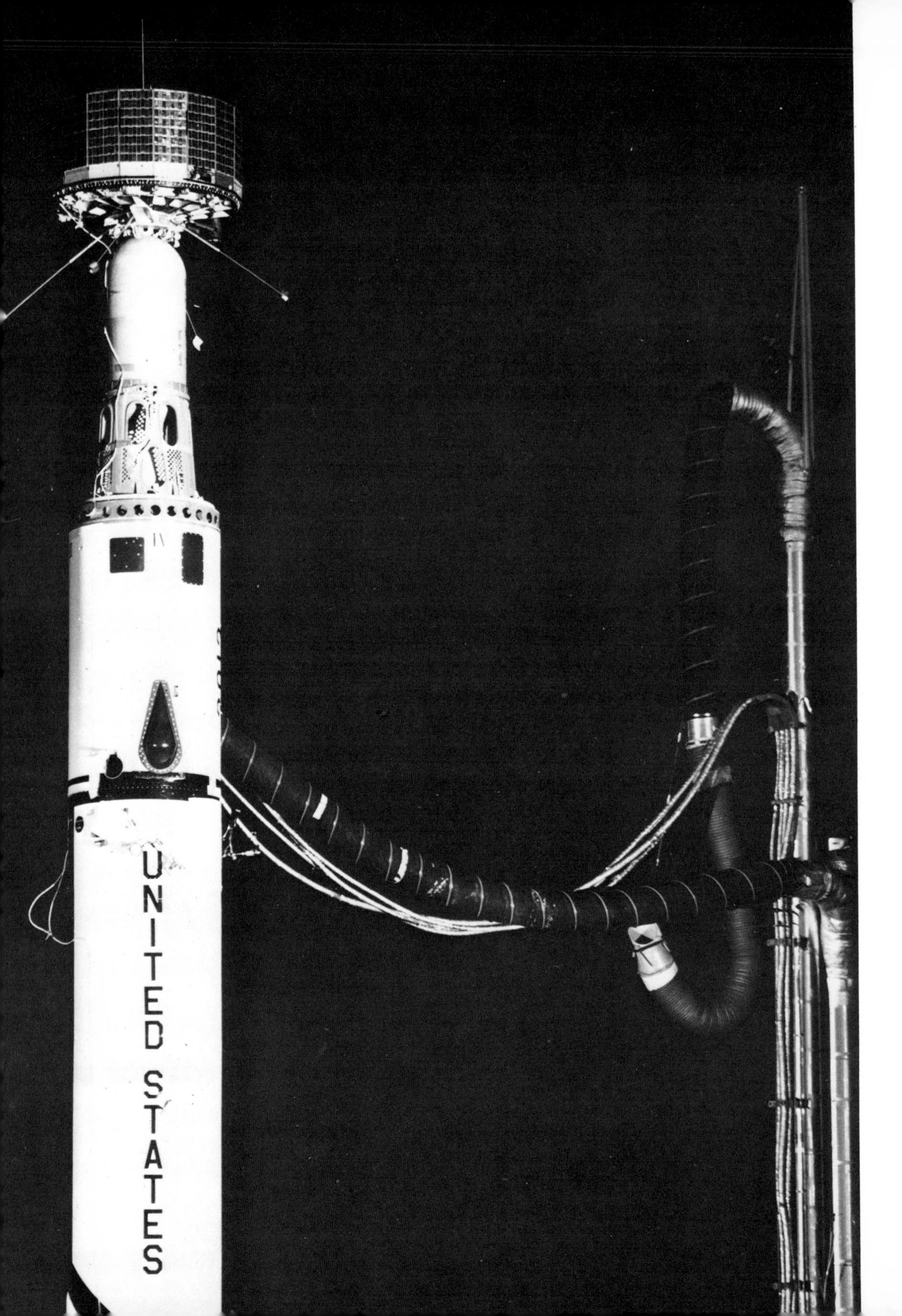
UNITED STATES

World Weather Watch

The balloon-borne radiosonde gave us a look at the weather from the ground up. But a "bird's-eye view" from hundreds of miles higher than a bird can fly is also very important. For a decade now, camera-carrying weather satellites have orbited the globe, giving us a new look at the troposphere—a view from above, as the moon men saw us recently.

Soon there will be dozens of satellites looking down and thousands of balloon-borne radiosondes looking up. At least, that is the weatherman's hope. As these portable stations sail the skies, they will "talk" to each other through their transmitters, compiling data even before it reaches the tracking station. Manned weather satellites may soon be in orbit, too.

Let's launch a weather satellite. The one in the photograph will orbit at about seven hundred miles from earth. It carries two cameras to photograph cloud patterns and storm formations.

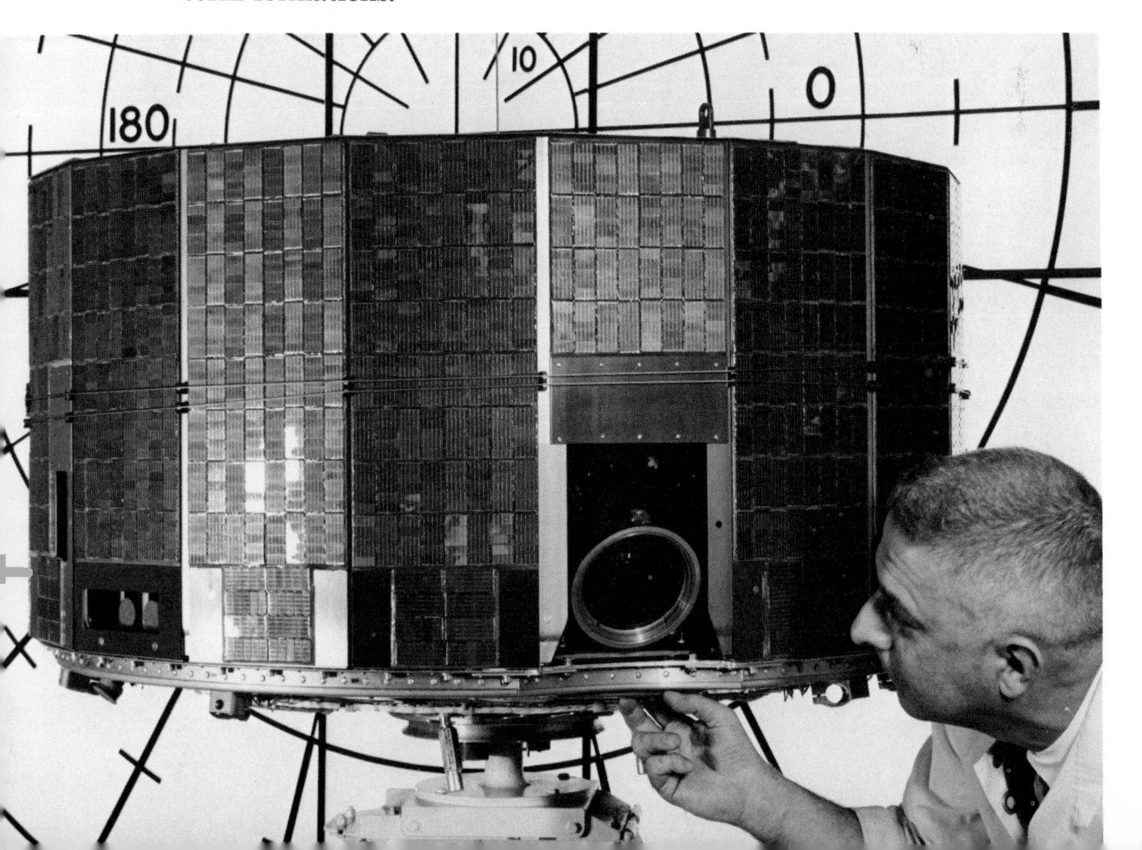

Blast off! A rocket boosts the satellite into space. They part company aloft. The cameras photograph 4.5 million square miles of weather around the globe. Any country can tap our satellite's data as the spacecraft passes over its station. That is, of course, if the station has monitoring equipment. Most countries have at least one such station.

Weather knows no political boundaries. The clouds swirl on the air above in utter disregard of the man-made divisions below. Because of this, the United Nations has a relatively new project. It is called WORLD WEATHER WATCH.

World Weather Watch enables weather data to flow about the world almost as freely as if the information were clouds and air. With more places on earth now watching the flow

of air and weather data, a perfect mathematical model may not be too far in the offing.

As our bird passes overhead, weathermen at Washington's tracking station get busy. Signals in the form of electronic impulses are picked up by an antenna, to work their way through the station's computers. The data is decoded and separated through an intricate electronic process in a minute and a half!

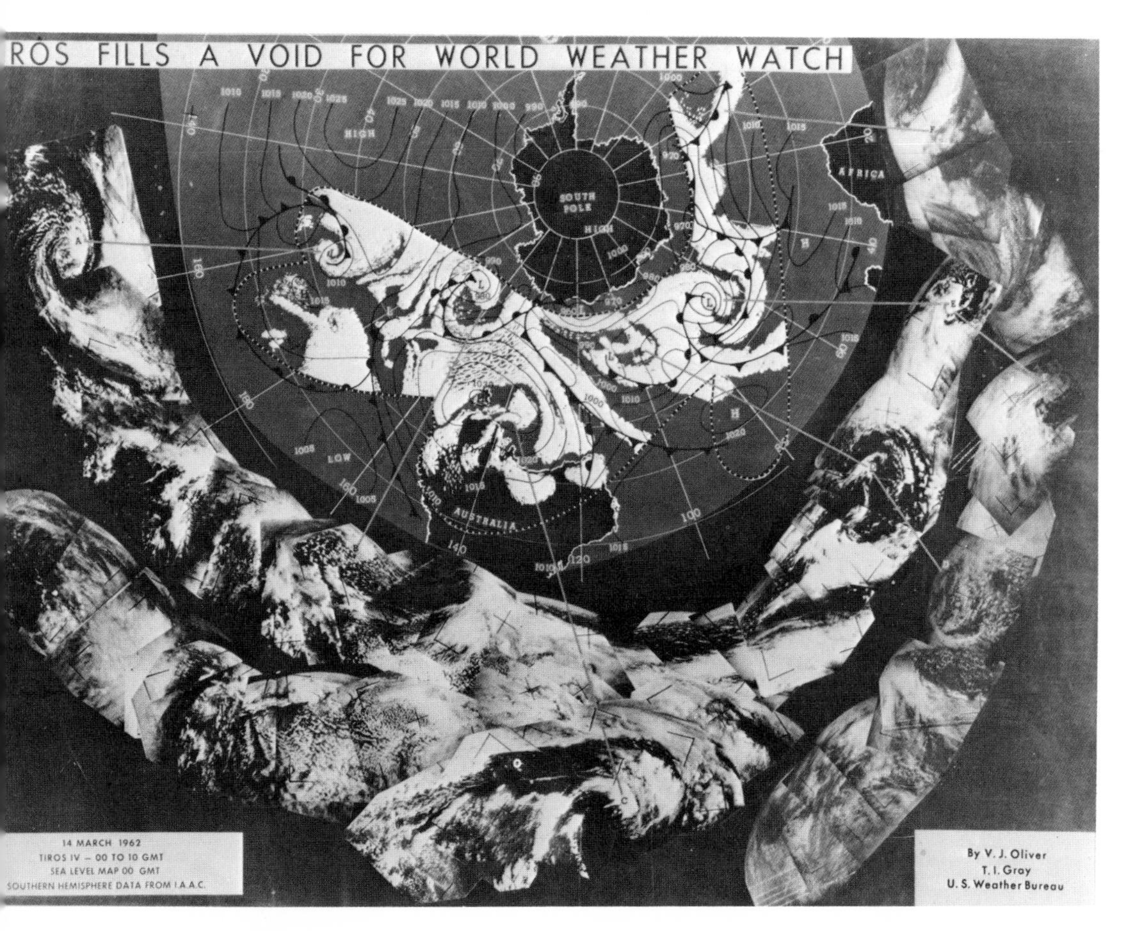

The signal impulses come in by way of the antenna to receivers at the tracking station. They are then translated into single-frame cloud photos which are matched up in a cloud mosaic like the one above. This shows cloud cover over the entire Northern Hemisphere on a certain day. Mosaics are used as a gross check on the forecasts which have been compiled from station and radiosonde reports. TV weathermen now use them to describe daily weather conditions across the entire United States.

Follow the Weather

Except as statistics, there is little as useless as yesterday's forecast. To make weather data the invaluable information it is, speed in the spreading of the news is essential. Telecommunications have proved to be very useful in this. Weathermen use teletypewriters and teletype receiver sets to send out and exchange data instantaneously.

Teletypes have many other uses, as do the computers to which some teletypes are hooked up. Newspapers use teletypes because speed is essential in news, too. A teletype is like a typewriter which is electronically hooked up to other teletypes on the circuit to which it belongs. For instance, all Weather Bureau teletype circuits feed information into the Weather Bureau's central station.

Weather teletypes have several different uses. Each station sends out an hourly local report. This information goes out on a small area circuit. It is used by radio announcers, pilots, commercial forecasting services. During weather disaster threats, special reports speed warnings to radio and TV channels, and thus reach the people who are threatened.

Each small circuit is hooked to a larger circuit, so that each station's hourly report ends up at all other stations throughout the country. A pilot flying from Boise, Idaho, to Buffalo, New York, gets current weather information about each city along his route by phoning the airport service. A weatherman checks teletype reports from the cities about which the pilot has asked. This enables the pilot to play hide-and-seek with storms, bypassing them, rerouting, or simply checking into a motel and watching them pass overhead rather than going on to risk his life by flying through bad weather. Aviation, in fact, is one reason for the great advances made in meteorology since World War II. Wartime bomber pilots needed weather information for survival and success in their missions.

Each station's report is pooled with all others coming in on teletypes at the Washington station. Here, the pooled readings are worked into maps and charts that show nationwide and worldwide patterns. Daily and three-day forecasts are based on these synoptic reports, which the Weather Bureau issues every six hours.

Probability forecasting is one fairly new way of using weather information as a basis for many kinds of decisions. The weatherman tells us what percent of a chance there is for a certain kind of weather on a certain day or for a longer time. If the forecast is a 90% probability of rain, better decide on an umbrella. Sixty percent might make you leave it home—if you are a gambler.

A cranberry grower in New Jersey sees that a five-day forecast shows a continental polar air mass moving in. It is colder than the surface over which it moves. There is a strong low developing to the west, and the probability of snow is 80%. It's a wise cranberry man who floods his bogs at this point. Flooding protects his crop from a frost that is very sure to come.

A roadside snack bar operator is ordering food for a late summer weekend. A strong cold front is moving in from the west. The probability of rain is 75%. He stocks up soups and sandwiches rather than salads and ice cream. On this unseasonably cool weekend fewer people will drive past his stand on their way to the beach. Those who do will be tired of summer fare. Knowing the weather, the man knows what to order. And knowing what to order, in what quantities, swells profits.

A pilot flying west to east can use hourly reports to stay well behind an eastbound frontal system. As he flies, snow-covered ground bears out each city's probability forecast in the wake of the front.

You are wondering if you should buy a ticket to the weekend ball game. It is Thursday. It has been raining for two days. The TV weather map shows that you are under an occluded front. There's a 35% probability of rain Saturday. Occlusions, you remember, don't usually last more than four days. You buy a ticket. Chances are good that you won't be rained out.

Since one man's playtime is another man's drought, and since you can't chant the rain away, follow the weather. On rainy days, visit a weather station with classmates. Work on a weather scrapbook. Track pressure systems, using the frequent radio and TV reports. Soon you will have a good sense of the patterns of movement that are part of the exchange of heat between sun, earth, air, and water.

Picture Credits

COVER, PAGES 12, 13, 14, 15, 16, 17, 21, 22, 24, 25, 26, 28, 35, 39, 43, 48, 54, 56, 57, 64, 66: Martin Iger

PAGES 6, 19, 33, 34, 36, 37, 38, 47: Cal Sacks

PAGES 8-9: Gemini Mission Chart, June 1966, USAF, Aeronautical Chart and Information Center

PAGES 10, 11, 30, 46, 51: Environmental Science Services Administration, U.S. Department of Commerce

PAGES 40, 44, 49, 52, 63: U.S. Department of Commerce, Weather Bureau

TITLE PAGE, PAGES 58, 59, 60, 61, 62: National Aeronautics and Space Administration

Index

Aerosols, 24, 41, 55

Air, density, 27, 29
  depth, 7
  flow of, 8-10, 27, 30-31, 32-40
  moisture in, 21-24
  pressure, 14, 27-31, 36, 39
  temperature of, 18-21
  weight, 27

Air masses, 28, 36-40, 48, 50
  continental, 37
  maritime, 37
  polar, 37
  tropical, 37

Air pollution, 55-56

Altocumulus, 38

Altostratus, 38

Anemometer, 35

Arctic, 50

Astronauts, 7, 8

Atmosphere, 7, 27

Aviation and weather, 65, 66

Balloons, weather, 12-16, 23

Barometer, 14, 29, 38

Cirrocumulus, 26

Cirrostratus, 26, 38

Cirrus, 26, 37, 38, 47

Cloud mosaic maps, 63

Cloud seeding, 53

Clouds, 8, 21-26, 37, 41
  altocumulus, 38
  altostratus, 38
  cirrocumulus, 26
  cirrostratus, 26, 38
  cirrus, 26, 37, 38, 47
  cumulonimbus, 25, 38, 43, 45, 47, 49
  cumulus, 25, 26, 47, 53
  nimbostratus, 25, 38
  stratus, 25, 26, 43
  stratocumulus, 26

Cold front, 39

Computers, 56-57, 62, 64

Condensation, 22-24, 46

Continental air mass, 37

Coriolis force, 32-34, 51

Cumulonimbus, 25, 38, 43, 45, 47, 49

Cumulus, 25, 26, 47, 53

Cyclone, 48-49

Dew point, 23

Doldrums, 50, 51

Drizzle, 22, 38, 43

Electricity, atmospheric, 41-42, 44-47

Electrosphere, 45

Equator, 19, 31, 33, 36, 37, 50, 51

Evaporation, 21

Eye of hurricane, 50, 52

Fog, 22, 24, 25

Forecasting, 8, 30-31, 48, 56, 63, 64-66
  long-range, 56
  probability, 65-66

Franklin, Benjamin, 8-9, 19, 31, 42, 44

Fronts, 37, 38, 39, 40, 47, 50, 67
  cold front, 39
  occluded front, 40, 67
  polar front, 36, 37
  warm front, 38

Gravity, 7, 22, 41

Hail, 22, 38, 43, 45, 49, 53

Haze, 25

High pressure area, 29-31, 40

Humidity, 21-24
  relative, 23

Hurricane, 50-52, 53

Hydrogen, 21

Hygrometer, 14, 23

Ice crystals, 26, 37, 41, 43

Instrument carriers, 12

Instruments, weather-measuring, 11-16

Ionosphere, 45

Isobars, 30

Jet stream, 34

Latent heat, 46

Lightning, 43, 44-47, 49

Long-range forecasting, 56

Low pressure area, 29-31, 40, 49

Maps, weather, 8, 9, 11, 30, 35, 65
  mosaic maps, 63
  synoptic maps, 11, 17, 65

Maritime air mass, 37

Meteorology, 41-42

Millibars, 30

Mist, 24, 25

Mosaic maps, 63

Nimbostratus, 25, 38

Northern Hemisphere, 33-34, 36

Occluded front, 40, 67

Oxygen, 21

Poles, 19, 31, 33, 36

Precipitation, 22-26, 38, 40, 41, 47

Pressure, air, 14, 27-31, 36, 39
  measuring, 14, 29
  sea-level, 29

Probability forecasting, 65-66

Psychrometer, 14, 23

Radar, 52

Radiosonde, 12-16, 20, 29, 59

Rain, 22, 25, 38, 41-43, 45, 49, 53

Rain-making, 53
Rain shield, 50, 52
Relative humidity, 23

Satellites, 11, 12, 59-61
Silver iodide, 53
Sleet, 22, 38, 43
Smog, 25
Snow, 22, 38, 43, 45
Southern Hemisphere, 33-34, 36
Space program, 7, 8
Squall, 39
Squall line, 39
Stratus, 25, 26, 43
Stratocumulus, 26
Sun, 18, 20, 51
Synoptic maps, 11, 17, 65

Teletype, 17, 57, 64, 65
Temperate zones, 19, 31, 34, 36
Temperature, 13, 18-21, 28, 29, 32-33
Temperature inversion, 55
Thermistor, 13, 20
Thunder, 37, 43, 49
Thunder showers, 38
Thunderheads, 47
Thunderstorms, 38, 43, 44-47
Tornadoes, 48-49
Tracking stations, 59, 61, 62, 63
Tropics, 36, 50
Troposphere, 7, 10, 11, 13, 19-20, 22, 34, 59
TV, 63, 64, 67
Twister (tornado), 48-49
Typhoons, 51

United Nations, 61
U.S. Weather Bureau, 10, 17, 48, 56, 64, 65

Warm front, 38
Water-in-air, see Humidity
Water vapor, 21-24, 41
Weather maps, 8, 9, 11, 30, 35, 65
Weather forecasting, 8, 30-31, 48, 56, 63, 64-66
Weather stations, 10, 13, 16, 17, 20, 30, 56
Westerlies, 34, 35
Wind, 28, 32-35, 39, 46, 49, 50, 51
  hurricane, 50-52
  jet stream, 34
  measuring, 35
  symbols, 35
  tornado, 48-49
  westerlies, 34, 35
Wind vane, 35
World Weather Watch, 61

About the Author

EVE MARIE IGER first became interested in weather when she accompanied her husband on flights across the United States, Mexico, and the North Atlantic in their light plane. As they flew over the countryside, she enjoyed observing weather conditions that bore out earlier United States Weather Bureau forecasts.

Mrs. Iger is also author of *Building a Skyscraper* and *John Brown: His Soul Goes Marching On*, both published by Young Scott Books.

A graduate of the Columbia School of General Studies, she is at present doing graduate work in literature. She lives in Briarcliff Manor, New York, with her young son, John.

About her other Books

Building A Skyscraper

"This beautifully designed and illustrated volume explains the logistics and science involved in the construction of a skyscraper. Ably researched, the text traces the creation of an actual 41-story building in New York City, from foundation to completion."

—*Library Journal*, July, 1967

John Brown: His Soul Goes Marching On

"A thorough, scholarly study of John Brown, interwoven with the tragic stories of his young sons, who fell victim to their father's fanaticism, and set against a solidly researched historical background."

—*New York Times*, April 19, 1970